BABA

BABA

HOW WE CARRY OUR FATHERS
AND HOW WE BECOME THEM

Viraj Rajendra Deshpande

LASAVIA
PUBLISHING

Published by Lasavia Publishing Ltd.

Auckland, New Zealand

www.lasaviapublishing.com

ISBN: 978-1-991083-31-9

Dedication

For my son, Aaroh.

Everything I do is either for you or about you. I'm with you even when I'm not. And also for the seven-year-old me on the cover. We did alright. Aaroh is a New Zealand citizen by birth. He has a New Zealand passport. Something his old man still doesn't have. It takes most sons decades to go one up on their dads. Mine? He just had to be born. It's poetic how his name came to me. The sun was rising over Auckland City. I had just finished my morning workout. I picked up a book I'd borrowed from work about using Māori wisdom to live in harmony with the land. I opened a random page. Read a random passage. And there, I found his name. "We all carry the potential for growth passed down from earlier generations. Trust the aroha of your ancestors deep inside you to realise your potential." Aroha—a Māori word that means love, compassion, respect, empathy. It stood out, not just because it was the only Māori word in the paragraph, but because I knew a similar word from home. In Sanskrit, Aaroh means rise, progress, ascent. And in that moment, I just knew. That's what I wanted to name him. A name that bridges two worlds. A name that belongs to both the boy from India and the boy from Aotearoa. Every time someone says his name, they'll be honouring two languages. Two cultures. Two histories. Two nations. As he grows, he'll get questions. Questions about identity, belonging, and what it means to have a finite existence in an infinite universe. I hope he goes on a journey to find those answers. I hope he grows into his name. But no matter where he is—in India, New Zealand, or anywhere in the world, I hope he feels at home in his skin. You were named by the sunrise, in the silence between two worlds. Trust the aroha of your ancestors. It knows the way home.

Contents

Foreword

With characteristic ebullience and good humour, Viraj Deshpande recounts his worldly experiences from his boyhood in India to adulthood in New Zealand. He writes well, his prose sharp and crisp. There's never a dull moment. He never lets the ball drop. He's one of those writers with ability to make writing look easy, creating a down-to-earth friendly, welcoming style that seems natural. I say 'seems' because you have to be a good writer to do this. He has a perceptive eye, and knows how to keep his narrative moving.

In the opening pages he writes about his early love for cricket with wry humour and characteristic directness. I smiled through these early passages, imagining the young Viraj getting up at two a.m. to watch Test cricket, holding his little finger in the hole where the on/off switch had once been to crank the family's ancient TV into life. The warmth and empathy with which he writes make identifying with him easy.

From early on Viraj fought against family expectations, to forge his own path in life, making the brave shift from Engineering (his family's choice) to strike out on his own as an independent cricket journalist. This struggle, and his subsequent success as a cricket blogger, are engaging. Viraj doesn't boast, but he has a charming way of getting us on his side and admiring him for his courage and resilience.

In 2017, he was accepted as a student in Auckland's AUT University to do a Masters of Creative Writing, which is when I met him, and had the pleasure of being his mentor. I soon learned that he was a person who wouldn't give up, who not just had the talent, but the determination to be a writer.

With lively prose, he brings to life his student days, the friends he made, and the remarkable story of his acceptance into the cricket community. There is also romance, but I'm not about to drop any spoilers. That's his story to tell. Suffice to say that his humour keeps up all through the book. In describing his first romance he comments, 'I was in fact so introverted, the first time I spoke with her it took so much out of me that I just came home and napped.'

While the tone is bright and the pace breezy, Deshpande doesn't shy away from deeper issues, and flashes of insight tend to slip slyly by: '... it's natural to get trapped in dogma in India where we have the world's highest per capita opinion.' With his student friends he deepens his understanding of colonialism and doesn't hold back from identifying 'colonial hangovers' in his beloved cricket.

It's not all smooth sailing, he doesn't shy away from identifying some negative attitudes towards India he finds here in New Zealand, and he recounts a family crises and subsequent premature return to India, being prevented from returning to NZ by the arrival of Covid 19, and the terrible toll that virus took in India. He describes all of this with typical robust honesty and simplicity.

This book is many things: an engaging tale, a tribute to cricket, a tribute to his family, an immigration story of an Indian man coming to live in New Zealand, and, perhaps, it is about the resilience of the human spirit, about how we can take the good and bad in our stride, and emerge stronger for it. Above all else, it is a good read.

I suspect that many readers will find this book inspirational. Viraj leads by example. You may fall on your feet or flat on your face, but you set out with courage, like Viraj, with your heart in your mouth and your fingers crossed, and like Viraj, you'll face squarely whatever fate has in store for you.

Mike Johnson
Waiheke Island
February 2025

Baba (Dad)

I had a headache last night when I went to bed. I slept well, full eight hours. And the headache was gone. It was a normal day. I woke up at 7:30. Took the dog out for a walk. Made coffee. Read the paper. Worked on my book. Had brunch. Watched a few episodes of Better Call Saul. Talked on the phone with a friend for a long time. Tried to take an afternoon nap, and failed.

By the evening, I started feeling kind of restless, as if something was missing. The last few months as far as peace of mind and mental health was concerned had been the best of my life. I had never felt more at peace with myself and the world, so this emptiness was kind of unusual.

Then I remembered the Test series starting tomorrow. When I was young, I used to be so excited the night before the start of any new India series that I couldn't even sleep. I used to visualize the toss, and sometimes the toss the next day would go just as I had visualized.

But these days, I only get excited before the start of a new Test series. I love Test cricket. And I love overseas Tests even more. So, the fact that India were playing New Zealand in a Test series in New Zealand should have made me restless with excitement. But why the feeling of emptiness? Then the memory hit me.

"Baba, the first series in our new house is going to be India versus New Zealand!" It was 2002 and the ten-year-old me was very excited.

My father just smiled.

We had just moved to a new house, in a swanky new suburb, a row house compared to our old flat in a not so good part of the town. It was a huge upgrade in all our lives. I, however, only cared about cricket. My world revolved around it, still does, no matter how much I try to deny it. I can skip the odd ODI or T20 but never a Test match. I am the most excited on the morning of a Test. It's like all my senses come to life.

There was no internet back then and we had to wait for the newspapers to see the schedule of the matches. The day it arrived, I was a bit concerned. *3:30 a.m. start.* I had started following cricket three years earlier and this was the first time I was going to watch it played in New Zealand. I had watched India play in Australia but the matches started at 5:30 a.m. That was bad enough, but 3:30 that was an ungodly hour. My mind started calculating: *3:30 a.m. start, 3:00 a.m. toss, that means pre-match show will start at 2:30 a.m.* That meant I needed to be up at 2:30 ideally.

There was also the concern about our TV. It was on its last legs, and we had lost its remote. There was a hole where the on/off switch should have been and my little finger was the only one small enough to poke through the hole, and I was the only one who could start the TV. You could say I was the king of the house, but who am I kidding, my family used me as a remote that could also fetch water, open doors and turn the gas off.

The thing was it used to take my little finger about ten minutes to find the button and then push it, and after that it used to take another ten minutes for the old idiot box to start. So my mind did some more calculations after taking that extra time in mind and this meant I needed to be up at 2:00 a.m. if I was to watch the pre match show.

My school was an afternoon school. So I could watch the whole days play and then head off to school. I would be sleep deprived and look like a zombie but who cared as long as I got to watch the cricket. However, my mum didn't let me set any alarms for 2:00 a.m. I had to be creative. I used the iron as my alarm. Iron gets cold. In winter it gets even colder. So I kept the iron at the foot of my bed hoping that somehow my bare leg will touch the ice cold iron at 2:00 a.m. and wake me up.

It worked. Not at 2:00 a.m. but at 2:30 a cold sensation on my left foot woke me up. I ran downstairs and started the process of getting the old TV started. Old bastard was taking even longer than usual. At around 2:55 a.m., I heard someone coming down the stairs. It was my father. Now imagine the scene from his point of view. You walk downstairs at 3:00 a.m. for a glass of water, and see your son, who is ten years old, sitting near the TV with his finger inside it, on a school night. Any other father would have been angry. But not mine. He knew why I was up, and I suspect he loved it.

"Kadhi uthla?" he asked. (When did you wake up?)

"Adich". (2:30)

And then the TV started just in time for the toss.

He watched the first hour with me, and then went back to sleep. He did say "zop lavkar" (now you too sleep) on his way back, but I knew he was just saying it because when he woke up the first thing he asked me was what happened in the game, and boy didn't I love telling him.

That evening around 6:00 to 6:30, our doorbell rang. And as soon as I answered it, the telephone started to ring too. I glanced past the man standing at our door to an auto with an open boot in which was a brand new TV. I asked the man to please wait and ran to answer the phone. *Someone bought a new TV* I thought, *and the man probably mistakenly bought it to our home.* I answered the call. It was dad.

"TV aala?" (Did they deliver the TV?)

"To aaplay?!" (Is it ours?!)

"Ho." (Yes.)

That was Dad. He liked surprising people. The day he bought his first bike he rode it from Shrirampur where he was working to Aurangabad where the family was, and surprised everyone. The day he bought his first car, same routine was followed, even Mum didn't know. And that TV was my surprise. From the next day onwards, I got an extra hour of sleep.

A year later Dad passed away. I don't have many memories with Dad, and almost every memory I have is cricket related. So whenever India tours New Zealand, and I set an alarm for 3:00 a.m. I remember that cold night in 2002 when Dad saw his ten-year-old son struggling to start the TV around 3:00 a.m. and bought a new TV that day.

After he passed away, people came to our house for months—people he had quietly helped, their stories unknown even to us. One of them was his cameraman from the local TV station. He arrived, sat down, and broke into uncontrollable sobs.

Through his tears, he shared something we had never known. Back then, the channel paid their crew in cash, each salary tucked into an envelope bearing their name. My father, he said, never once kept his own envelope. Every single time, without a word or acknowledgment, he handed it to him.

It's been over twenty years since he passed away but I still feel him around me. In family and friends and colleagues and kind strangers. There are glimpses of him everywhere. Because knowing the kind of man my father was, I'm certain not even death could stop him from looking out for us.

His days would start at 4 a.m. as he headed to read news for the City Morning Radio. He would then do his nine to five as the manager of a reputed Bank. Then he would come home for a bit before heading to the local TV channel office as he was the face of the seven p.m. news. Then he'd come home, have dinner with the family, ask everyone about their day while also cracking the most hilarious jokes and then sit down to write his column for the local newspaper. In between he'd field calls from friends, from family, from the Lions Club he was the secretary of, or from the organisers of a big cultural festival he was hosting.

He was everything everywhere all at once. If you were lucky and saw him in person you understood why people couldn't get enough of him. He had a magnetic aura. He'd walk into a room and you'd feel his presence. Heart of every party. Funniest person in the room. Even though he was extremely busy we never felt like he didn't have time for us because when he was with you he was with you. Undivided attention.

It was Dad who introduced me to cricket. The game had such a big presence in my house that it was hard not to get sucked into it. Apart from being a banker and a newsreader, Dad was also an active club cricketer and a cricket columnist in the local newspapers. So there was always cricket on our TV and cricket books and magazines lying around the house.

My first memory of watching cricket on TV is the 1999 World Cup played in England. The first match I saw was India's first match of the world cup against South Africa. India made 253, and lost. But I was hooked. That 253 stuck in my seven-year-old head for a long time. It was the first cricket score I knew. I'm glad it stuck because thanks to that 253 and the power of Google, years later I could search and find the scorecard of that match.

I watched as many matches as I could of that world cup. It wasn't hard because summer holidays were on. During the world cup we went to Shimla – a popular hill station in the northern part of India – on a family trip and I remember asking Dad before booking the hotel room to make sure they had a TV with cricket channels. I did not want to miss my first India v Pakistan match. The room had TV, and of course India won.

The first book I read was a cricket book, *Idols* by legendary Indian cricketer Sunil Gavaskar. It was the Marathi edition of the book, but the title was still the same only written in Devanagari. I did not know the meaning of Idols because of my age. To put it like Mr. Gavaskar, I was still in single digits. Then I converted one into two and read my second book, *Sunny Days* also by Gavaskar.

Dad used to call from his office to ask the score. I never used to tell just the score. I used to tell him the whole scorecard, how many runs scored by each batsman, how many balls faced, fours and sixes hit, the detailed bowling figures of every bowler and also whatever incidents happened like if Tendulkar was given out wrongly, as would often happen. The funny thing is I knew that all by heart, I did not need to look at the screen.

That process would be repeated when Dad sat down to write his newspaper column. I would sit beside him to provide the statistics from the match. Some nights I would write my own account of the day's play and ask him to publish mine too along with his. He used to laugh it off. Once, however, he didn't. During the 2003 World Cup he published my little tit-bits in the local newspaper. The name was mine, the photo was mine, but the words were his. I was over the moon. But I did let him know that I was disappointed that he didn't publish my actual words. Again he laughed it off.

By then my relationship with Dad had transformed into a cricket relationship. I would wait for him to come home from the office so I could tell him how I fared at the school, not in studies but in cricket. Did I score any runs, did I bamboozle the batsmen with the googly he had recently taught me or did I take a spectacular catch. He would listen with genuine interest.

That conversation was my best part about every day. I still remember the joyous pride on his face when I told him how, playing my first competitive game in school, I hit the first ball for a six and the ball broke the staff room window (The last I checked, they still haven't fixed the window!).

I used to bombard him with cricket questions as I loved to get his point of view on things. And his views would inevitably become my views. Like how winning Test matches abroad counts more than winning at home, how Sunil Gavaskar's thirty-four Test centuries scored without a helmet against the fast bowlers of that era rank higher than that of Tendulkar's.

He was a great admirer of Ganguly. As Ganguly, along with John Wright gave his generation, a generation who had gone through the trauma of the nineties where India lost everything abroad, a team that they deserved, a team that could win Test matches outside India.

It was only fitting that the last Test match Dad watched, before a brain stroke took him away from us, was a Test at Adelaide in 2003 where India managed to register their first win on Australian soil in twenty-three years. They really did give one of their ardent supporters an apt good bye!

I was eleven, too young to realise the enormity of the situation. For a few months after that every time the phone would ring during a match my heart would skip a beat. Cricket became even more important as it became my refuge, my escape from reality. It was also my only connection with Dad as most of my memories with him were cricket related.

Every time a world cup came around, I remembered the world cups of 1999 and 2003 which I watched with him. Every time India toured Australia and I got up at 5:00 a.m. in winter to watch, I remembered how he used to wake me up, carry me in him arms to the couch in the living room, throw a warm blanket over me and turn the TV on. Watching cricket, I somehow felt closer to him than at any other time.

So that's what I did. I watched cricket. Be it Tests, ODIs and later T20s. India matches, non-India matches, domestic matches. I didn't care. I watched it all. It was easy to watch One Day Internationals; I just needed to skip school for a day. But it became difficult for Test matches that would go on for five days. I could not skip school for five days. So I skipped school on the couple of days on which India batted. The toss would happen at 9:00 a.m. for a Test in India, three hours before my school auto would come to pick me up. So if India batted first, my school auto invariably wouldn't come. At least that's what I used to tell Mom. If India bowled first, I had more time to fall sick the next day.

I watched so much cricket that I learned more about life from cricket than actual life. Well, it could not have been any other way as I watched so much cricket, I had no actual life. Thankfully there is no other sport that teaches as much about life as cricket does. The first and the most important thing I learned from cricket was the English language, as the commentary was only available in English at the time.

Cricket was my window to the world. I learned that New Zealand is a small but beautiful country that regularly punches above their weight. And the Kiwi people are a friendly lot, unlike their hostile neighbours across the Tasman Sea – the Aussies. Waiting for the match to resume after a fine sunny day had given way to rain and more rain at Manchester, I understood England's favourite pastime –talking about the weather. I learned that Sri Lanka is a proud little island that knows how to make the most of its limited resources. Reading about South African cricket was when I first read the word apartheid, and then learned about Nelson Mandela.

"To follow cricket is to be a student of life." These are the words of Sambit Bal, the editor of ESPN Cricinfo. British writer, Harold Pinter went a step further, memorably describing cricket as "the greatest thing God created on earth —certainly greater than sex." The teenage me who anyway wasn't getting any action thought Pinter was being too dramatic with this statement. But now I'm old enough to have had my share of experiences, I can make a rational observation that Pinter's statement, to use an old British term, is bollocks. But I can see why Pinter chose sex to compare with cricket. In Test cricket too the actual action happens just for a few minutes and then absolutely nothing happens for days on end. I Feel sad for Pinter's partners though.

Almost every Indian kid first dreams of becoming a cricketer. I was no different. And it's only when he or she realises that they aren't good enough, do they think of other career options. Even if you have the talent it is difficult to pursue cricket as a career in smaller towns. I was a small town guy minus the talent, so becoming a cricketer was out of the equation. However, by then I had realized that my serotonin levels were highest while watching cricket. So I had to figure out a way that I would get paid to watch.

I had an end goal in mind. Very early in my life, the cricket bug bit me so bad I knew I was going to be watching it for the rest of my life. Might as well make a living off it right? Capitalism and all that. So as I had an end goal in my mind, I just worked backwards. Which profession will pay me to watch cricket? Journalism was the obvious answer.

Apologies for this Personal Attack

But like most of us, for a while I too got trapped in dogma, living with the results of other people's thinking. And it's natural to get trapped in dogma in India where we have the world's highest per capita opinion. After my tenth standard board exams, I too took the science stream (just cos all my friends were doing so) and was preparing for the CET (the entrance exam to get into engineering colleges in India) when the realisation hit that I don't want to become an engineer.

And that's it, one fine day I decided I was not going to appear for CET. Announced it to my family. They were concerned of course. Mum called up my successful engineer *mama* (maternal uncle) to have a chat with me and change my mind. Even my friends reacted as if they had seen a ghost when I first told them about not doing CET as

I didn't want to be an engineer. The thing my family and friends said was, "Ok don't do engineering, but just do the entrance exam." No harm, right?

So, I did the exam, got decent marks and actually was eligible to apply to a few decent enough colleges.

Now they said, "Just do engineering, get the degree and then do whatever you want."

"Fair enough," I said.

I completed engineering and sat in some of the campus interviews just cos friends were doing it although I had no intention of getting an engineering job. And voila, a company actually offered me a good job with great pay for my age. Now everyone said you're still very young, you have lots of time. Work for a few years save enough money and then start your own business. Fair enough, I said and started working.

This is what happened to most of us. But that's not what happened to me. So here is what actually happened. When my *mama* came to talk some sense into me, I just didn't budge at all. I am nothing if not a stubborn asshole of the highest order. So, my family eventually gave up. I was so sure about it. I remember reading an article in a supplement of a local newspaper. The supplement was called 'Oxygen' and the article in Marathi was titled *"Mag apan ka jagto?"* (Then why do we live?).

That article was basically about how the majority of the people get trapped into dogma and then take a path they didn't want just because someone else told them to or just because they were afraid to go against the grain. That article was a huge turning point, a wake up call for me.

It made me realize that our work is where we spend most of our life. Do we really want to do work which we do not love just for the sake of money? The answer was a firm no. I decided to take the road less travelled. I decided to pursue journalism.

By now my family and friends had pretty much accepted the fact that I was in fact going to follow my heart. They were in the *"Ye sunne wala nahi hai"* (He's not going to listen) stage which is just before the *"ladka gaya hath se"* (He's on the path of destruction) stage or the *"hume pata tha tu life me kuch karega"* (We knew you'd do something great in life) stage depending on the outcome.

My late dad did have a journalism degree, but he pursued it as a hobby while he was working in a bank. It wasn't his career. As no one in my family had pursued journalism as a career, one of my uncles took me to get guidance from a well-known journalist and journalism professor of my city.

I sat in his cabin all excited, thinking that he'd appreciate me for choosing a different path that too at a young age (I was seventeen at the time). What transpired was the exact opposite. He said, and I might be paraphrasing a bit here as the incident happened long ago: "Don't come into journalism just because everyone else is doing it. First get a degree in any field and then pursue a master's in journalism with the thought of becoming a journalist in the field you already have a degree or education in."

In hindsight, that was a pretty sound advice. But seventeen-year-old me didn't go there for sound advice. I went there to hear: "welcome to the club, son. Yes all your friends are losers". So his first line felt like a gut punch. Here I was thinking, I'm following my heart, going against the grain, taking the road less travelled etc. And the man here just turns the tables on me saying don't do it cos everyone else is doing it?! Um hello, uncle, no one else I know is doing it! Why do you think we came here?! I left his office more confused than I was earlier.

How to Lose a Girl in 10 Days

But the sad part was, I couldn't shake his advice off. Neither could my family so they convinced me to first get any basic graduation degree and then go for masters in Journalism as was suggested by the veteran professor. So I went for BSC (IT) degree. On the first day of my college, we were sat in the class and the professor was just telling us about the institution, the course etc when someone asked the most important question asked in terms of a career in India: *Sir scope hai kya?* (Sir is there any scope?).

Let me first paint a picture of our professor. He was the carbon copy of Patrakar Popatlal, a funny loser character on popular Indian TV Show TMKOC with a pencil moustache and ridiculously arched eyebrows. But, our professor if that's even possible was even thinner with a face only a mother could love and doing a job which must have been the last option on his career plans.

There was a brief pause. You could feel the anticipation build. Our patrakar Popatlal doppelganger professor looked at the guy, smiled and said: "I'm from this same institute. I did this same course. It worked out well for me right?" Nervous laughter echoed across the hall. My mind had only one thought. If I'm going to turn out like this guy, kill me right now. Do it!

Apart from that professor, our institute had a bit going on for itself (inadvertent grade cricketer reference if you know you know). It had the biggest and the best campus in the city. But that's not saying a lot as the city was Aurangabad. It had arguably the best college canteen which served arguably the best jumbo sandwich.

But the biggest attraction of our college like any other college was a girl. You know how in every college there is that one girl who everyone is after. Seniors, juniors, freshers, professors, canteen uncle, staff, and even some of the girls. She was that girl!

She once went to watch her friend play chess, and that was the first time in the history of chess happening at the college that the indoor stadium was full. Word got around that Ritika (name changed because her father as I later learned was a political bigwig) was there and that was it. The first time I saw her, she was standing outside of our class. Our classes had these big glass walls so you could see outside and vice versa.

As soon as I saw her, I nudged my friend, as that's what good friends do. He said some expletive ridden excitement and then nudged the guy beside him; a minute later the whole class was looking outside.

She saw me. I smiled. She smiled. My friends saw it. Now this is the romantic version of putting a handkerchief on a bus seat. I still don't know why she smiled, maybe because I was the only one smiling. The rest of the boys just had their mouths open. Can't blame them though. A few minutes later her friends came, and she was gone.

The next day the same thing happened. Her class used to finish half an hour before mine. And she used to wait for her friends to come sitting diagonally opposite of me as we stole glances.

She was way out of my league. So much so that she was the Indian

Premier League and I was a Pakistani cricketer (Pakistani cricketers aren't allowed to play in the Indian Premier League). No chance at all I thought. However, I was to learn soon that there's a brief window to land an out of your league girl after she's joined your college. It is the first couple of weeks. The first couple of weeks not everyone knows her yet. And most of those who do are too scared to approach her. And she is also kind of lonely, looking for new friends and secretly getting anxious that no one has asked her out yet. Those two weeks are your only chance.

Of course, I didn't know all this when I spoke with her. I realised it over the course of the next month. The first two weeks, they were magical. She used to wait outside my class, we used to steal some glances and that gave me enough confidence to just speak with her, which I did soon. And the next thing you know we were walking the campus together. I was giving her a chocolate every day. We were having lunch together in the canteen, and I was finally the guy I always wanted to be, the average looking nerd with a goddess. I could actually hear the *what does she see in hims* whenever we used to hold hands while walking. Even I didn't know what she saw in me. Only later, I realized it was those first two weeks. Another thing that worked in my favour was she only spoke in English. Not even Hindi, and Marathi was out of the question. So that ruled 99% of the boys out.

The first time I spoke with her, I had a realisation just how out of my league she was. She was from Mumbai, was the daughter of a big politician. She was hot AF, rich AF, extrovert AF. And I wasn't any of those things. I was in fact so introverted, the first time I spoke with her it took so much out of me that I just came home and napped. Yes. Only introverts know this feeling. One day she told me some guy is calling her constantly and she was worried. I said let me handle it. She sent me his number and I called him. And I went all *maa-behen* (using all the mother sister related expletives) on the guy. I didn't think this through at all. Because I called him from my cell phone. He was not only from my college, but he was from my class. He figured out who I was.

And the next day when I went to the class that guy, Irfan his name was, sat behind me and he made sure every maa-behen gaali (abuse) I

22

gave was returned with interest and while he was doing so I glanced at my friends sitting near me and those fuckers were knowingly ignoring that such a thing was happening. So just like that I lost the girl, and, in my mind, also my friends. I didn't want to be on the wrong side of Irfan and his gang of 15-20 boys who I had to spend the next three years with in the same class. So that was it for me and Ritika.

She soon found a hot AF, rich AF guy and moved on. Now here's the funny part. I have no contact with Ritika today, but me and Irfan ended up being Facebook friends. Not even kidding, I wish him on Eid every year and he wishes me on every Diwali. You know what they say bros before those garden tool things.

Harsha Bhogle? Who's She?

My college also had a journalism department. I had taken admission there for a six-month course of TV journalism. Yes, that's what it was called. Not multimedia journalism, not video journalism but TV journalism. We had classes twice a week, and had professional journalists teaching us. That course was an important little part of my life, which reminded me I hadn't given up on the dream yet.

However, that journalism department was fairly new and a six-month certificate course was highly unlikely to get me a job. And shit got real when one day I saw a familiar face in my journalism class. It was my *nukkad ka paan wala* (Street vendor selling mouth fresheners at a corner shop). Yes, you read that right. My *nukkad ka paan wala* who was about the same age or maybe a little older than me was doing the same TV journalism course.

That was kind of a wakeup call for me. Alarm bells started ringing. That *nukkad ka paan wala* at least has a family business to go back to if he doesn't get a journalism job, what do I have? Whatever peace of mind this course gave me was now gone. Add to that I was feeling increasingly out of place in my BSC (IT) class.

I just didn't feel like I belonged there. Some of the classes were interesting, I had made few good friends. I also performed well in the first semester exams but I wasn't happy at all. I was just out of place. I felt like a duck learning to climb a tree just because a bunch of monkeys around him were doing so.

Then one day I decided this was it. The article "*Mag apan ka jagto?*" (Then why do we live?) was still fresh in my mind, and I didn't want to be like one of those people who get trapped in dogma and are scared to go against the grain and end up living the life they didn't want just because "*Log kya kahenge?*" ("What will society say?").

So even after scoring 80% in the first semester, I quit BSC (IT). Goes without saying my friends were shocked. "You are good at it, why are you quitting," was the most common reaction. I just couldn't do something just because I was good at it if my heart wasn't in it. And that is something they didn't understand. Thankfully my family did, and they were pretty supportive. And that's all that mattered.

So, I decided to apply for the journalism graduation program at Symbiosis, Pune. Pune was the closest big city to my hometown. As a part of their admission process, I was asked to write why I want to become a journalist, and those shortlisted will be asked to come to Pune for group discussion and personal interview round. I wrote a piece titled "Why I want to write".

This article convinced my family that I had some talent, and they were willing to support me and see where that talent took me. Mum in fact liked it so much she took a bunch of print outs and took it to her office. I really liked it at the time but now I can't even read it.

Anyway, I sent this article to Symbiosis as part of my application to their journalism graduation programme, and they liked it. I was among the select few called up for GDPI round to Pune.

There are moments in your life where the decisions you take

impact you for the rest of your life. Good, bad whatever the decision might be. I made the decision of not going to Pune. Around that same time my elder brother had secured a place in one of the colleges in Pune for his masters degree, and if I also went there Mum would have been alone here. And it was just my graduation, I could always go away to a better institute for postgrad I thought and stayed at Aurangabad and took admission to a Bachelors in Journalism course in Aurangabad.

That turned out to be a huge decision. Because had I gone to Pune and studied in Symbi, I would have been a good journalist, and gotten a really good job no doubt. But I would have been a slave to the company with no time for family, and to do anything creative or out of the box.

So I was an 18 year old guy at home in Aurangabad with a good broadband internet connection, and lots of free time on my hands, and who had just discovered he could write. So that's what I did. I wrote. And I sent those articles to as many editors and publications and websites as I could.

I even sent one to Harsha Bhogle, a famous cricket commentator. I still don't remember how I got his email ID. It was an article titled 'What Makes Cricket Great' and the answer to it, I argued, was the Indian cricket fan, and not Tendulkar or Bradman or the BCCI. Harsha wrote back. Yes, I was even more surprised than you are. He wrote "nice Viraj." Yes, that's it. But those two words were encouragement enough for the teenage me to keep writing.

When I got Harsha's email, I was so overjoyed I shared it with everyone. I called up my girlfriend. I could barely contain my excitement. "Harsha Bhogle replied to my article!" I screamed. "Wow great, who is she?" This was her exact response. And just like that all my excitement was replaced by bewilderment. To be fair to her no one in her family followed cricket and at the time she had a friend (girl) named Harsha.

Having a Start-Up Before Start-Ups Were Cool

'What Makes Cricket Great' was also the article that led me towards Binit Singh, the first person who changed my life, and without whom none of the things I have done so far would have happened. The article impressed Binit so much he hired me to write player profiles and match reports for the 2011 World Cup. It was a dream job – first gig getting paid to watch cricket, a step in the right direction.

It also meant I had to go to Pune but as it was only for the World Cup my family was cool with it. Binit Singh was a tall, skinny fellow with a voice like Amitabh Bacchhan. He worked from his flat in Pune by himself and his website had a turnover of around 15 lakh (a lakh is 100,000 rupee) at that time. But the bottom-line is he was earning a living from his website, which was pretty good. He offered to pay me

5000 rupees per month plus 100 rs for every piece of mine that got published.

I was nervous. I was excited. I was happy. I was actually getting paid to watch cricket. My living arrangements were sorted. My cousin who was working overseas had a flat in Pune where his sibling stayed alone. And as that flat was really close to my 'office' I stayed there. The matches started at 2:30 p.m. and would go on till 10 p.m. I needed to be in the office by noon, and then, as I didn't have my own vehicle, there and was dependent on public transport, I used to leave for home before eight, and finish my work from home. That was my daily routine.

Binit was a really nice guy. Pretty chilled out, and he was quietly proud of what he had achieved with his website. It was fun working with him. The only thing I had to be careful about was not mentioning to anyone in that apartment or housing society that I was coming here for work. As it was a residential building and our guy was running an office from there.

A few weeks passed. It was going good, but deep inside I had a strong feeling that I wrote better than Binit. I couldn't shake it off. And if I already wrote better than him what was the point of working for him? But I stuck around there until one day when the final nail hit the coffin. It was during one of the non-match working days. I had the task of updating the pages of cricket grounds. I saw that the Adelaide Oval page had a completely wrong photo.

Adelaide Oval is the most beautiful cricket ground in the world. It has everything. Grass banks, white picket fence, seagulls on the field of play almost all the time, and it's not circular. It has its own dimensions: big straight boundaries, short side boundaries – the same short side boundary Rahul Dravid hit to achieve one of India's finest Test wins in 2003. Who can forget *that* square cut, then the kiss of the badge on the cap. It was also the last Test match Dad saw. And Adelaide Oval was the most beautiful cricket ground even before day night tests came. Now day night tests have taken it to another level. No ground can compete.

You now know how much Adelaide Oval means to me, and how it must have hurt to see a photo of a random ground there instead of the picturesque Adelaide Oval. What made it worse was my boss didn't care. He didn't fucking care what photo there was. "Well, as long as it's a cricket ground," his exact words. To give you an idea about how much that comment hurt me imagine you are a huge Tabla fan, and work for a music website. Your boss posts a picture of Malinga on the dedicated Zakir Hussain page and when you ask he comes up with the lamest excuse: "I don't care, same hair".

At that moment I knew my boss was a businessman masquerading as a cricket lover. I was, and still am, an absolute cricket romantic. Cricket tragic. At that time, I had no life outside cricket. I used to watch cricket on TV all the time, read cricket books, wear cricket tee shirts and my favourite band was the Duckworth Lewis Method: an Irish pop band which mainly creates cricket songs.

There is so much romance in cricket. So much artistry. So much poetry. Each session is a stanza, each over, a verse. Most (not all, sorry Graeme Smith) cricketers are artists. Look at footage of Damien Martyn caressing the ball for four through the offside and tell me that's not art in its purest form. The moment when ball meets Martyn's bat is so perfect, it's just like when you're listening to a musician playing an instrument and they get into that zone when every note is perfect and the instrument obeys the musician so much it almost feels like a part of their body.

It is the same feeling you get watching a Damien Martyn push through the offside, or a Yuvraj Singh flick off his pads – the batsman, the bat, the ball all become one and produce art. Calling it sport would be a disservice to the show on display. It is art. And it should be played only on grounds that do justice to the artwork. Because the ground adds so much.

Now imagine the shot at the Adelaide Oval. It is a good length ball just outside off stump. Martyn just plants his front foot near to the pitch of the ball and just blocks it, albeit opens the face of the bat at the point of impact just a touch. The bat doesn't move an inch after contact is made with the ball. The ball however races past the fielders in the thirty-yard circle, then towards the seagulls near the boundary. The seagulls all fly in unison to avoid being hit. It is a sight itself. And then it reaches and stops at the foot of the white picket fence. Art.

A few days later, my mama, yes the same mama who Mum had called home to put some engineering sense into my journalistic brain, invited me home for lunch. He used to live in Pune too.

So while at his place, I mentioned the thing about me thinking I already write better than my boss. And he just said why don't you start your own website then? I thought he was joking, but apparently, he wasn't. He had already registered a website for one of his business projects so he had an idea about domains, hosting and how to get your .com basically.

I had no clue about any of that. I just knew how to write, and even that I was learning and in no way was it a finished product. But I was so excited by the idea of my own website, I said, "let's give it a crack." I registered my own website the next day. The next week, I resigned.

I had no clue at all about how to run a website. But it wasn't a spur of the moment decision although it may seem like it. The teenage me actually really thought this through. My logic was let's work on my own website for the duration of my graduation (I was in the first year of a three year course). If my business starts generating revenue by the end of my course, all good. If it doesn't, I can always go for postgrad like rest of my batch mates.

So in February of 2011, I registered criczest.com. I didn't tell Binit I was quitting, I told him I had exams and I would need to go back home for a month or more. But he knew. Of course he knew. And he in fact took it well, and said one of the nicest things. He said, "You're too good for this job. I was hoping you'd realize that a lot later than this though."

So that was it for my first ever job. I quit in the first month with a dream to start my own thing. I didn't know what I was getting myself into, probably that's why I got myself into it in the first place. I often tell friends, "if I knew at the time how hard it was going to be to successfully run my own website, I would never have quit that job in the first place."

But ignorance is indeed a bliss. Sometimes it helps to not know the challenges you are going to face beforehand, and face them head on when the time comes. Always better to cross a bridge when you get there rather than fretting about it the whole way. That's one of many things I've learnt from my super mum.

Writing 2000 Pages of Content

So here I was back at home in Aurangabad. I had a start-up on my hands way before it was cool. Even a month ago, I didn't know what a domain was, now I had a website of my own. I used to edit in Dreamweaver at the time, then I graduated to Visual Studio before permanently shifting base to Wordpress.

I don't think I have ever worked as hard as I did for the first three years of criczest.com. I would literally either be working or thinking about work every minute I was awake. Because, A - I was working for myself and I was loving it, and, B - I had something to prove, that I did the right thing quitting that job.

I was writing new content all the time, when I wasn't writing, I was researching for what to write next. When I wasn't doing that, I was researching new designs for the website or any aesthetic changes or any improvements or ads. I was basically a hamster on that wheel running non-stop.

In the first three years of criczest, I wrote 2000 pages of content on my own. If you consider each page was around 500 words, some were longer some shorter but if you consider 500 words to be average then that means I wrote around 10 lac (one million) words in those three years, the equivalent of writing twenty five short novels. Stephen King, who?

In the prime of my youth from the age of 19-22, while others were going out having the time of their lives, I was staying in creating content for free. I remember one IPL season, I think it was the 2012 one, that for every single match my work was to write a preview the day before the game, do live scores during the game, write a review post game, and also a create a post featuring best tweets about the game. So, for a single game I had to do four different posts. Double-headers meant I had to do eight different posts for the day, and the preview of the next day's game/games. IPL has 60 games in 50 days usually, so in those 50 days in 2012, I created around 250 pages of content all by myself.

Even though I wasn't making any money yet, didn't mean I took my work lightly or not as seriously. I took it as seriously as any job or successful business. It was a priority. I never skipped a match. I knew if I did not take my work seriously, no one else would. My friends and family soon understood to not schedule anything on match days, and if they did they understood if I missed it. And all of this was before I made a single dollar from it.

Many good things happened even when I wasn't making money through my website. Good things which gave me confidence and assured me that I was on the right path. As a young writer I was filled with self-doubt, the constant voice in my head questioning if I'm good enough. It used to only go away for a brief moment right after I wrote something good. However, it did go on a longish holiday whenever I got published in a reputed organisation or got feedback from a prominent person.

Harsha Bhogle was the first famous person to read my writing and say nice thing about it. And I mean nice literally as that's all he wrote to me. *Nice, Viraj*. But Murali Kartik was more generous. During the 2012 IPL, I had started a new section on my website in which I wrote about incidents happening during the games in a more dramatic way. One such write up was about Murali Kartik and his face off with Dinesh Karthik. It was titled "I'm the best Kartik around" and I actually pulled Murali's leg in it multiple times.

I'm the best Kartik around!

Murali Kartik is a proud old fellow. Takes great pride in his slow left arm orthodox, tweets about his achievements from the past, says in interview that he is still the best left arm bowler in the country and backs it up on the field not with his tantalizing left armers, but with egotism to put any left arm spinner in sight out of the park. As he did to Ojha in Pune's first match of IPL 2012, hitting a six and four in consecutive deliveries of the sorrow face Hyderabadi.

Kartik's I'm the best beep the rest attitude isn't restricted to his bowling, he also feels that he is the best Kartik around. And when he got a chance to prove it against the Mumbai Indians' Dinesh Karthik, he wasn't going to let that slip and what transpired was full of drama.

Bowling the 11th over with Dinesh on strike, Murali was a bomb waiting to explode. Anything could have ignited him, even a back foot defence, let alone what Dinesh did, coming out of the crease and pushing the ball straight to covers. That was the limit; you don't leave your crease when Murali is bowling, not even for a run!

Murali politely warned Dinesh saying son, you don't step out to legends, if you do it one more time, there will only be one Kartik in cricket after that! However, the delivery which followed wasn't even half as good as the warning- a rank long hop gleefully put to the boundary by Dinesh! The sin of all sins was made; the limit had been crossed big time. Somebody had to pay and we all knew who it will be.

The very next ball turned voraciously and beat Dinesh, who was out of crease as Uthappa stumped him ending the family friendly part of the match right there. As with smoke coming from his ears and eyes red with flare, Murali bumped his 24" chest with irritating arrogance saying I'm the best Kartik around and in between didn't forget to make a few references to the female members of the other Karthik's family.

I actually shared this kind of embarrassing write up with him on Twitter, and to my surprise he not only replied it seemed he really liked it. As you can see below:

Kartik Murali
@kartikmurali

@criczest Haha,it's very funny..well written mate

6:54 PM · 25 Sep 12

As I was creating unique, quality content, getting Adsense account was a breeze. The challenge was maintaining it and not doing anything stupid, as Google has pretty strict policies. I made a dumb mistake. I actually told my friends and family that I get paid when someone clicks on the ads on my website.

So, I don't know whether it was one of my friends clicking on my ads multiple times in a day or myself inadvertently clicking on my own ads while working, but my Adsense account soon got banned for invalid clicks. And just like that my bubble burst. I remember that day. I bawled my eyes out. I was sad, I was not sad I was crushed. And that day also I got an important realization. Not a single person I know knows anything about my work. I had no one to turn to, take advice from. In my first major professional/life crisis I was just completely alone.

I didn't know what to do now. Did my website get banned too? Or just my email address? Can I apply for another Adsense account for same website with different email? Might as well give it a try. I read some stuff online about what to do in this scenario and there were suggestions of using a different address other than the one you used for the banned Adsense account. And it was that time I found out that you can rent mailboxes. I rented a mailbox in Hyderabad for three months. They collect your mail and then mail it back to you on your own address.

But it just didn't feel right inside. So I just created an email id in my mom's name and applied for Adsense giving her name, Email id and phone number. A few anxious weeks later I got that email from Google welcoming me to Adsense. As it turns out Google doesn't ban the website, they just ban the email id/ phone number.

The great thing Google still does is they give a 500 rupee voucher to everyone who signs up for Adwords. Now Google Adwords which is now Google Ads is a platform through which you advertise your business on Google search and various other websites that display Google ads.

October 2013 was a huge month for me. 12th October I got published in ESPN Cricinfo. 14th October I got published on Wisden India website. The cricinfo piece was about an ODI I went to between India and Australia in Pune. But the Wisden piece was a straight from the heart talk about Tendulkar's impending retirement. It was titled: "Let's not rush through Tendulkar", and Wisden India called me a 22-year-old cricket romantic in the author's bio. Getting published in two of the best cricket publications was a sign enough that the writer in me was on the right path.

The Idea That Made Me $50,000 Richer

But the biggest moment of October 2013 wasn't about that. It was about that 500 rupee voucher from Google which showed me there was light at the end of the tunnel. By this time I had been working on criczest.com for 2.5 years and I hadn't made a penny yet. I was in the final year of my graduation and I desperately needed something to ensure my family support my decision to continue with the website rather than going for a masters.

I created a page which displayed all the information you needed about buying tickets for that India v Australia series. It was created specifically to use that 500 rupee voucher. Then I created my first Adwords campaign.

It worked. I actually made substantial profit from that campaign. I was happy and sad at the same time. Google only gave one voucher, now what? But my girlfriend was a great sounding board for literally everything, and we had a thing going on where if I was stuck, I'd just come up with solutions while talking to her. The funny thing is, even though I was the one coming up with the solution, the solution wouldn't occur when I was by myself pulling my hair out at the desk. I had to be talking to her and explaining her the situation and then something would click.

But this time it was the other way round. She just said why don't you spend your own money on these campaigns. The first did actually make you profit right? She was right. Well even if I had made 100 rupees it would have been profit considering I didn't actually spend anything on the campaign. But I made much more than the 500 I "spent." So I spent a further 500 from my own pocket.

The best thing about running an online business or a website is there is no time delay between your investments and the returns on it. Like it is in a traditional businesses. Take restaurants for example, the owner could spend a fortune renovating the restaurant but whether people like it or not he won't know till it's all done and open to the public. On the other hand, Adwords and Adsense both report and track your expense and income respectively live, so you have the option of pulling the plug on a campaign if you're incurring losses. So, it was all looking good for me to try out an Adwords campaign with my own money, well technically my mum's money, but whatever.

After that Australia series India were going to South Africa for a tour. I had created a tickets page for the Australia series and that was the page I had run a campaign for on Adwords. But now as it was a tour of South Africa and my majority audience being from the Indian subcontinent, I couldn't do the same tickets page and subsequent ad campaign as it's of no use to my market.

I had to come up with something that I could do or campaign irrespective of the location of the match. What is it that cricket fans want most apart from match tickets? Then it hit me. Two glorious words. Also the most searched cricket keywords on the internet: live cricket. Cricket fans want to watch cricket live, on their laptops, tablets and mobile. And they want to know which TV channel is showcasing the series so they can subscribe to it.

If I was Thomas Edison, the thought of monetising live cricket was my light bulb moment. So I created a post titled India's tour of South

Africa: Live telecast details. And then I created a pretty simple text ad campaign. It cost me 3306 rs and brought 13752 visitors to my website. Those visitors helped me generate a revenue of just over 9000 rs. So I had made a handsome profit of 6000rs. This idea to monetise live cricket was a new lease of life for my business. I continued running similar campaigns for the next year, which was 2014. That year my website generated a revenue of just over 4 lakh rs.

The timing could not have been better. I was in my final year graduation. Some of my engineer friends were getting placed, and I had generated similar revenue from my business to the packages they were getting offered. It was enough for my family to continue to back me and allow me to continue what I was doing rather than opting for a masters or looking for a job.

Another stupid thing I did was, as my Adsense was in my mum's name. I had connected her bank account to my Adsense so my monthly payment were deposited in her account. And it was her salary account too. We really didn't think it through. When the payments started getting big and she got worried it might raise a few eyebrows, only then did we opened my own business account.

La La Land

I still remember what Ashlesha (name changed) said when I got my first pay cheque from Google.

"How lucky I am that I get to see you become something, and be a part of the ride rather than meeting you when you've reached somewhere. I get to see you grow." She had said a similar thing when my first article got published almost four years ago. She believed in me, more than I did in myself.

The funny part was I believed in her more than she did in herself too. She was an artist through and through. Whatever she did was art. Be it actual art or the poise and grace with which she carried herself. She'd find artistic ways to do normal things, where I, on the other hand, was more focused on getting things done. She cared deeply about how a particular thing is done. It had to be perfect. It had to be creative. It had to be cute, and it had to be a bit funny. Basically, a reflection of her own self. She'd spend hours, sometimes days, just to get the cloud at the top right corner of her painting to look a perfect colour. I used to call her "Lady Picasso."

So, when Lady Picasso was working in a bank when she was just twenty-one, I had to get her out of there. She wasn't happy. She didn't belong there. Her talent was too precious to be wasted. But she was also a bit scared to leave a stable government job most people would give their right arm for. Even talking to her parents about it was a scary prospect for her.

Thankfully for Lady Picasso, I had a great relationship with her parents. But I didn't know just how much they trusted me until one morning I received a call from her mother. She was extremely distressed. Her younger brother (Ashlesha's favourite uncle) had passed away suddenly that morning, and they had to go but they hadn't told Ashlesha yet, and her mother trusted me to come over, stay with her till they're back, and break the news to her when I felt it was appropriate.

Ten minutes later, I was at her place. She was told that her uncle was not well and has been taken to the hospital. She was a bit worried but she didn't suspect anything was wrong. So, she was okay, which meant I had time to think about how I wanted to break the news. It was around 8.00 a.m. when I went to her place. I was there till late evening. Around early afternoon is when I told her that he was no more.

She was obviously broken. I told her that if she wanted, I could take her to see him for the final time as there was still some time left for the last rites.

"No," She said, "I can't see him like that."

We just sat there in silence. After a while, when the tears had stopped and she had drunk some water, I asked her again, "Do you still feel the same about not going?"

She hadn't changed her mind. She loved him too much for her last image of him to be from the day he died. "I'll go in the evening after he's been cremated," she said.

So we just sat there in silence until she remembered something about her uncle from her childhood. She'd share the incident and go quiet again before she remembered something else. I knew my job was to not to say anything, just listen and be there for her as the tragedy slowly sunk in. I drove her to her uncle's place in the evening before returning home.

The things she and her parents shared about her late uncle made me feel like he was quite similar to my dad. Her mum said that he once got out of his car to see what was causing the traffic jam ahead, then realised the traffic signals were not working and there were no traffic police either. So, he took it upon himself to act as the traffic cop for the next half an hour and cleared the traffic jam. That sounded a lot like something my dad would have done.

While my eyes were dry throughout the day, while riding back, the tears were flying, I mean literally because the wind was so strong the tears were flying back from the corners of my eyes. I felt bad for those riding behind. The incident her mum shared hit too close to home. This was also the year that I'd officially spent more of my life without my dad than with him.

I was dreading this milestone growing up because I could no longer console myself with the thought that my time with Dad was still more than without him. Now I console myself by saying I'm still younger than what my dad was when he passed away. But I know in a few years, I'm going to be older than my dad ever got, and while that is a terribly sad thought, I know in my heart that it's something he would have pulled my leg about, so it's kind of funny.

That was a bit of detour, but it shows how much her parents trusted me because I needed every single bit of their trust when I went down on one knee and proposed to them to please let their artistic daughter leave her high-paying, stable government job and follow her heart.

One of my friends had asked me not to help her leave her "nine-to–five."

"If you both follow your hearts, who'll pay the bills?"

I just said, "no wonder you're single."

Thankfully, her parents didn't think like my friend, and the bird was freed from the cage. And then it was my turn to watch the bird fly. And fly it did. In fact, it flew so far away, we were no longer together.

It wasn't the bird's fault. It was my own. When the bird needed me the most, I wasn't there to stand by her. I was too self-absorbed in my own problems and thoughts. I lived in my own cricket bubble and was yet to step out of it and into real life. But she'd been doing this real-life thing all along.

She knew how hard real life was. While she was my first girlfriend, she had experienced a bad relationship before, and knew what a precious thing we had. I didn't know any of that. I was stupid. She did try hard though. I know she tried with every ounce of courage she had to hang on for both of us. I couldn't meet her halfway. She didn't even expect halfway. Even two steps would have been enough. I lacked the courage to take even one step.

When I did get the courage to go all the way, it was already too late.

"I just want something normal now. I can't risk doing this again." she said.

I didn't know what she meant at the time. I understood it later. It's true girls mature way earlier than boys. What we had was too good to be true, hardly believable. It was straight out of a fairytale, and she didn't have the energy to do that again. She wanted a normal relationship. Something that won't look straight out of a movie but would look normal, everyday, so she could live peacefully.

Even during the difficult period of our separation, she was thoughtful and full of grace. Whereas I, on the other hand, behaved like a toddler throwing things out of his pram. Not even caring about the damage I was causing to those around me, those who loved me. So, she cared about them for me.

One of the last things she told me when I was having a depressive episode, trying to come to terms with our break-up, was to just look at my mum and live for her. " Look how much grief your mother has already gone through in life, yet how strong, happy, and kind-hearted she is. Do you want to be the reason for more grief in her life?"

That slapped the sense right back into me.

"I'm living for my parents too," she said.

One of the less spoken parts about a relationship ending is how it also brings to an end a few additional relationships in your life. Like the one I shared with her parents, two of the nicest people I've ever met.. I genuinely enjoyed spending time with them. I'd even give them a visit when Ashlesha wasn't home. I genuinely cared about them, and they always made me feel welcome and a part of their family. They watched me grow up. We were 18 when we started dating. They saw my transition from an 18-year-old awkward boy to a 27-year-old awkward man.

They knew the dreams I had, and as I ticked off some of them, it was a shame I couldn't share it with them. I know she felt the exact same way about my family too. We both achieved all the dreams we saw while we were together, except the one that brought us together.

Like Elon Musk Inviting You Home and Telling You to Buy Bitcoin in 2012

Thanks to that success in 2014, I was one of the select few Google Ads publishers from all over India who got invited to a Google seminar at JW Marriot in Delhi in mid-2015. Well technically my mum was invited, my AdSense account was still in her name remember. Obviously, mum couldn't go so I sent Google an email on my mum's behalf asking if a colleague of hers could attend the seminar on her behalf. No problems they said. And I was off to the capital.

I was about to experience my first flight, my first Google event, and my first and only time (so far) getting kidnapped. Yup, just Gurgaon things. I was a nervous wreck before leaving. I was an introvert at that time. So first ever flying experience, first ever Google event that too at a posh hotel was all too anxiety inducing for me.

The event was on 27th Feb 2015. My website had a really good 2014, and an even better start to 2015. At the start of 2015 there were huge events back-to-back; India played a ODI tri series in Australia also involving England. Then there was the ICC Cricket World Cup followed by the IPL. There was an ODI between India and Australia on 26th January 2015, which is republic day in India. It was an innocuous game. Nothing special about it yet I had my most successful day. That day my website generated over 18,000 rupees in AdSense earnings.

It was an early indication of the potential of my business. And it also provided me with a really important business lesson, which I still bear in mind. The way my business works is I advertise it on Google search, get traffic from there to my website and then generate revenue from the ads on my website.

But usually there is huge competition to get your ad on those first few Google search result spots. And you have to sometimes shell out extra bucks compromising on your profits. However, as world cup and the IPL were set to follow this innocuous tri series, most of my competitors, I realised, were saving money for those two events. So I went all out and I got those top few spots at a much cheaper rate and that's how I made more profit than I'd ever made till that time.

Coming back to the Google meet, it exceeded my expectations and not only because the food was just delish. It was a full day event, and various experts and industry leaders came on stage and gave insights. I still have my notes from it. It was there that I got to learn that the organic search is gone. Khatam. Tata. Bye bye. And the future is mobile.

At the point where my business was, those two lessons were worth their weight in gold. I was so excited with that information, I even went and asked one of the Google reps how many publishers are at this meet. "Eighty," she said. So okay eighty people know. They'll spread the word to at max 500 publishers. Ok let's assume a 1000 publishers in India know about this. That is still a miniscule number compared to how many publishers there are in India.

Organic search is dead. Future is mobile. What intel. What a headstart. This was almost like Elon Musk inviting you home in 2012 to eat delicious food and then saying oh by the way buy bitcoin. That shit's the future. I had goose bumps seeing that presentation about how the future is mobile, and then I had orgasms thinking about the things I can do with it. The costs I would save, the money I'd make.

The first thing I did after returning home was work on making my website from mobile friendly to completely made for mobile. Google reps were right. A deep dive into Analytics confirmed what they were saying at the seminar. Over 90% of my traffic was coming from mobile devices.

Another domino effect of that was as I wasn't getting any desktop traffic I could save a lot of costs by completely targeting my Adwords Campaign to mobile devices only and not waste money on showing my ads on desktops and tabs. I also switched to WordPress around the same time. And I have been using WordPress ever since.

So all these changes contributed to me not only saving money on campaigns but earning more even from a similar number of visitors than what I had had earlier. As my website was mobile friendly, the pages loaded super-fast and ads were easily visible on the screen, that resulted in an increase in the click through rate (the percentage of people clicking on the ads), which resulted in more advertisers bidding for ad slots on my website thus increasing the CPC (cost per click) and in turn my revenue multiple times for the same amount of traffic.

My RPM (Revenue per thousand impressions) was around 400 before these changes. After that it was around 1000. To put it in simple terms, remember how I made 18,000 rupees on Republic day 2015? If I had made these changes before that, that day for the same amount of traffic I would have made around 45,000 rupees.

2015 turned out to be more successful than 2014 business wise. Now my website was a serious revenue generating business I could rely on. It was kind of the perfect business model. I was working from home so there was no rent, maintenance or even petrol costs. Since I started earning in late 2013 there wasn't a month I didn't get a pay cheque from Google. So, stability was there. The family was happy. I was basically living the dream.

In August 2011, when I was in the sixth month of running my website, I had stumbled upon a blog post online which gave me a lot of hope and a good road map to ensure my business was on track even when it hadn't started generating revenue yet. I'm sharing it here. This roadmap is exactly how it turned out for me.

What does the path to success look like? A typical scenario

The path to success is a very slow upward curve. Success is the result of a long period of small improvements.

I know you want real numbers and exact times and amounts of work. The following scenario is what I've experienced, and what I've observed among friends and colleagues who've endeavoured to make money on the internet. Note that this scenario is for someone who puts in serious effort, not just a weekend here and there.

The first month: You're excited about creating your website. It's new and interesting. You work hard, creating the basic pages of the site, and writing your first articles. No one comes to your site, but that doesn't bother you.

1m – 6m ("Website Winter"): The initial rush of enthusiasm has worn off. You've put in a lot of work, but you're still getting almost no visitors. A few random people are coming in through obscure Google searches, and through the few links you have. You're making 0-50c a day from a few clicks on your advertising, or maybe you've sold one product.

Website Winter is the most common stage at which websites die. Not knowing what's ahead, many webmasters become despondent at this point, and give up.

Regardless of not getting any worthwhile results, you stick with it anyway.

6m – 12m: You write lots more content for your website, and the size and quality of your site improves significantly. You start to get a few good links from other sites, and you show up on Google for some low-traffic searches. You break through the 100-visitors-a-day mark. The first trickle of money has started coming in. It's under $10 a day, but it's something you can see, and can improve.

1y – 3y: Your website is now a serious resource, with a significant amount of high-quality information. You've had a small but tangible stream of income for a while now, and you begin to make your site more efficient. You start marketing your products better, or maybe you get better at deploying advertising on your site. You test new sources of revenue. Your profit starts to multiply.

You break through the 1,000 visitors a day mark, and your site churns out $100+ a week.

You know how it all works now, and you can see that your $100 a week could soon turn into a liveable wage.

You keep working on your site, and your income eventually hits the point at which you can live off it.

3y – 5y and beyond: Having succeeded at making money online, many of the people who get to this stage actually stop here. They just sit back, and live off their website. It's been hard work, and they've already reached the most important milestone. You can't blame them.

If you choose to continue here, you find it becomes easier and easier to make money. You've become very adept at marketing, internet commerce, and website technology. With your comprehensive knowledge of your field, you can see new and greater opportunities, or new websites or ventures.

You become one of the very small number of people to achieve serious wealth online.

If you can start a website, and stick with it even after the initial rush of enthusiasm has worn off, it's your ticket to serious financial reward. As long as you get past the 6-month point, it's probably going to make you some money.

This last part about if you can start a website, and stick with it really kept me going. I stuck with it even when it wasn't generating revenue. In fact I worked the hardest around that time. The result was my website became a foundation, a solid base which enabled me to follow my heart and see where it led me. I had the monthly income part sorted but there was more to life than just a monthly pay cheque. And I wanted to explore that.

Kidnapped in Gurgaon

Oh I almost forgot the second most exciting part of that trip, the kidnapping incident. I laugh about it now but *thodi der ke liye waha pe goti muh me tha* (A famous saying in Hindi which literally translates to for some time the balls were in my mouth. Basically an extreme state of nervousness and panic.). If you know you know. After I finished the meeting around 5:30 p.m., I left hotel and went outside to look for a cab,auto, or anything really to take me to the airport. It was early 2015, so Ola and Uber weren't yet a thing, at least not in my world.

As the hotel was on the outskirts, closer to the highway, there unfortunately weren't any taxis or autos around. I stood outside for a ten to fifteen minutes to no avail. I should have gone inside the hotel and asked them to get me a cab to the airport but my middle class ass stopped me from taking the overpriced hotel cab.

But while I was waiting a white Omni van drove into view. In hindsight white Omni should have been my first clue. It is literally *the* kidnapping car. I asked for a lift with my left arm extended and thumb sticking out, and the car pulled over. I noticed that it was pretty old car and the driver wasn't the most trustworthy looking person.

"Where to," he asked

"The airport," I said. "I'll give you a hundred ruppees if you take me there.

The man shrugged. "Ok, get in.

I went to get in the back.

"No no," he said sit in front.

I got in and pulled out onto the highway. He started chit chatting, and not the kind of questions you ask in small talk. He asked about how many houses my family has and how much land they own. That was my first clue that something was wrong. Then on the highway instead of going straight to the airport he took a turn into Gurgaon. Gurgaon, for those who don't know, is famous for its crime rate.

I had started to panic. "Why didn't you go straight?" I asked.

"I have to do some work here" he replied, "don't worry you won't miss your flight." Missing my flight was the least of my concerns at that point, and uncomfortable silence filled the van.

We stopped near a house and three very shady people hopped into the backseat.

Yeah, I was sweating. At that point we should have taken a U-turn and gone back to highway on our way to the airport, but no we kept going further into Gurgaon. I was shitting my pants, thinking of ways to escape. I saw a shop in the distance where quite a few people were standing. And when he slowed down near a speed breaker or a pothole, I just jumped out with my bag in hand and ran towards the shop. He stopped the car got out and hurled abuses at me. But I didn't care. I was safe. I went to the shop, sweating bullets, had some water, and calmed myself down. Then the shopkeeper showed me a bus stop nearby from where I could get a bus to the airport.

I Have a Dream

It was 2016. I was 24 and living the dream of getting paid to watch cricket at home. Life was good. I also used to spend a lot of time on Twitter. During a twitter scrolling session, I came across a Delhi based company who needed someone to write humorous articles for them. I applied just because I found their application form hilarious. Turns out they found my application hilarious, and lo and behold, a week later I was making some extra cash writing stuff like '10 Andaz Apna Apna dialogues for real life situations' or '10 hilarious Paresh Rawal dialogues for corporate life':

> *When someone mistakenly dials your extension:*
> *Kutriya saala, dekh ke number dial kar! (Hera Pheri)*

When you mistakenly dial someone's extension:
Arre baba wrong number hai toh uthati kaiko hai re? (Hera Pheri)

When the boss asks you to brief a client:
Pehle mereko yeh samjha... ki isko samjhana kya hai (Hera Pheri)

So in my spare time I wrote humorous pieces for them. And some went properly viral. They liked my work so much they wanted me to shift base to Delhi and work full time for them. But there was a small problem – *Delhi dur thi, but mujhe thoda aur dur jaana tha* (Delhi was far but I wanted to go even further).

I wanted to pursue masters from outside of India. It was either Masters in Journalism or Masters in Creative Writing. I pondered on it for quite some time. The mind was with the former but heart said the latter. I followed my heart, no surprises there.

Now I knew what I wanted to do, it was just a question of where. My options were limited. I wanted to go to a cricket playing nation because all my work was cricket related and it really wouldn't make any sense doing a 60,000 word cricket related writing project in say, Germany. So, I realistically had three options: England, Australia, and New Zealand. All the options were good but considering the post study visa structure and the costs etc NZ was the clear front-runner. And I have been in love with New Zealand ever since I first saw it on TV in 2002 when India toured there.

In New Zealand, three universities offered the Masters in Creative Writing course I wanted to pursue: the University of Auckland, Auckland University of Technology, and Victoria University in Wellington. I wanted to go to Wellington not only because it was known as the coolest little capital in the world by Lonely Planet, but because of one of the most beautiful cricket grounds in the world – the Basin Reserve.

To apply, I first had to clear the IELTS (International English Language Testing System). It's really a basic exam and I cleared it without any trouble. The next part was the tough one, preparing a twenty-page writing sample and a Statement of Purpose for the university application. I wrote the SOP and the twenty-page sample and sent it away to all three universities, hoping to get a call back from Victoria University in Wellington. I heard from Victoria University first, but it was a rejection letter. Followed by another rejection from the University of Auckland.

Now only Auckland University of Technology remained. They were a new university compared to the other two but my programme there was in the top 1% of the world. AUT did show interest in my application, thanks to my mentor Mike Johnson, who I later learned was adamant about getting me there. There were a few things that needed to be worked out before my admission was final.

As my project wasn't a typical creative writing project, the university had concerns about the exegesis. An exegesis is a critical explanation of a text. I didn't even know the spelling of exegesis at the time let alone what it meant. No wonder the other two universities rejected me. But Mike helped me work out the technicalities so the admission board were satisfied and just like that I was going to New Zealand!

Now, Auckland doesn't even have a dedicated international cricket stadium. They play cricket primarily in a Rugby stadium, Eden Park, also known as the smallest cricket ground in the world. Hell even I could hit a straight six there. But Auckland is still 1000 times better than Aurangabad.

There was a specific reason I wanted to go study in a cricket playing nation. I wanted to become an umpire. I know, a twenty-four-year-old thinking of becoming an umpire is a really sad thought. But there were a couple of strong reasons behind it. First, I just love the game. So much I wouldn't mind standing in a field counting to six and waving my arms around a bit for eight hours in the sun watching other people play.

And secondly, in my head I was a cricket writer. But to become that in other people's heads too I needed to make a name for myself in the game, which people will trust, and gain actual experience on the field, learn more about the game and if possible, go into the record books. You know only players and umpire's go into the hallowed record books of this weird old game. And let's face it. A by-line which says 'written by Viraj Deshpande New Zealand Cricket Umpire' looks a lot better than 'written by Viraj Deshpande a random cricket fan from India'.

When it was certain I was going to go to Auckland, I went on the Auckland Cricket website and got the email ID of their umpiring in charge, Doug Cowie. Doug Cowie was a former ICC umpire who officiated in Test matches all around the world and also officiated in the 1999 edition of the ICC cricket world cup in England.

Remember that famous Tendulkar hundred in the 1999 World Cup against Kenya? To those uninitiated, Sachin Tendulkar's father passed away during the 1999 WC in England, and Tendulkar came to India for a few days to be with his family during the tough time, and then went back to play in the World Cup. That Kenyan match was his first game back. And he scored one of his most emotional hundreds, and looked up at the heavens acknowledging his late father. It remains one of the most poignant moments in Indian cricket, and guess who was the umpire at that game, Doug Cowie. But Doug isn't famous for that. Doug is famous as the man who gave one of the most shocking decisions on the cricket field. It is a viral YouTube video titled: *Batsman misses out ball by a metre, given out caught behind. Worst umpire ever!* Doug is often teased about that dismissal, but he's a sport.

I emailed Doug and told him that I was a cricket nerd through and through. Who else could think of becoming a professional umpire at twenty-four right? To be honest I didn't expect a reply, but I got one the next day! Doug was very welcoming in his email. He said, *just let me know once you're in Auckland.*

My mum didn't beleive I would umpire there. She didn't tell me at the time but she told after I had done few matches.

"You didn't even umpire here," she said, "how could you umpire in a different country?"

My mother had a point. I had tried to become an umpire in India but the Indian Cricket Board is so negligent as far as developing new umpires is concerned, I couldn't even appear for a level 1 exam, which they don't even hold for years on end. It's really tough trying to become an umpire in India. The pay is also terrible unless you reach first class level. There is politics, and you are not treated properly. All sorts of things work against you.

But it is the exact opposite in New Zealand. There is a proper structure in place, and a fixed pathway for aspiring umpires, the pay is 10-20 times better depending on the level you're umpiring at, and most importantly you are respected, and I can say all that from first-hand experience.

So I had a place secured in my course and a job I could do while there, now I just needed to find a place to stay. Many of my friends who studied abroad, went in packs, a pack of friends that either know each other from before or met each other during their study abroad admission process for which they go through an agent. The pack does everything together, including renting a place to stay. My agent also sent me a few contacts of other Indian students who were going to study in Auckland so I could rent a flat with them.

But what was the point of going abroad if was going to continue to live the same life and hang out with the same people as I did in my home country? That wasn't for me. Studying abroad was a once in a lifetime experience. I feel many Indians go abroad to hang out with other Indians. I did not want to be that way and I went a few extra miles to make sure of that before I picked a hostel to stay in Auckland. But don't get me wrong I love India as much as anyone and I also have really close Indian friends who I met in New Zealand. And yes, I understand the security of having your community around you in a foreign country.

It was not difficult to find a place. Thanks to the internet and various groups and chatter on social media, I got a fair idea about the neighbourhoods and where the Indians live in Auckland. I had two options, either to stay with a family as a paying guest, or homestay, as it's called or to live in a hostel. As my classes were just once a week, I thought, as I was going to be spending a lot of time at home, it was better live at a hostel with people of a similar age for company.

After weeks of searching, I found a hostel that fit all my requirements. It was called Rocklands Hostel, and was in Epsom, one of the most beautiful and leafy neighbourhoods of Auckland. For the first few weeks of my stay, I was the only Indian guy there. It was perfect in every way. It was a bit costly, but you can't have it all.

But before I got there, I had to get through my first international flight, first layover, and first immigration experience alone. Up until then the furthest I had flown was 90 minutes. The first flight, Mumbai to Singapore was six hours, and second, Singapore to Auckland, was eleven hours! My introvert overthinking self couldn't sleep at all the night before my flight.

The Mumbai to Singapore flight was ok. My family came to drop me at the airport, and it was familiar territory. But when I landed at Changi Airport in Singapore all by myself the reality of how alone I was and how hard this was going to be, struck me. It struck me so bad I think I had legitimate panic attacks and lost count of how many times I went to the bathroom. Everything was overwhelming.

I sat anxious at the gate waiting to board my flight to Auckland. There was a British girl sitting beside me. I think she noticed I was kind of anxious and she started a conversion.

"Hello" she said.

"Hi" I said half nervous and half relieved.

We just talked for over half an hour, just general small talk. But that small talk and just talking with another person and sharing what you're feeling is such an underrated blessing that we take for granted. That talk took care of all of all my nerves. I became comfortable, confident even, and the anxiety disappeared.

"Where are you sitting," she asked when we were about to board.

"The upper deck," I replied

"What you mean upper deck?" She gave me a confused look.

"This is a double decker plane, don't you know?"

She didn't. Even I didn't. My best friend who's a pilot had told me about it when I booked the tickets, so during web check-in I made sure I booked a seat on the upper deck.

It was my longest flight yet, eleven hours, but it was nice and comfortable. And the food was great. I even managed to get a few hours of sleep in. The anxiety was long gone now. Replaced by a similar feeling of excitement. I was about to land in New Zealand. New freakin Zealand! Over a year of hard work and preparations had led to this moment.

First Night in NZ I Had to Call 911

Our flight landed at Auckland Airport. I disembarked from the aircraft, entered the airport building, and joined the queues for immigration. They had quite a few immigration officers sitting behind a glass cabin doing their job. I had to get in line with any one of those officers. There was a big Māori guy, an elderly white lady, a young white man, and an older brown man.

I wasn't going to take any chances. I went and stood in the queue that would lead me towards the officer that looked most like me. I was a bit nervous standing in that line. You cannot be of brown skin and not be nervous in an immigration queue. My turn came.

"Hello," said the immigration officer from behind the glass.

I said a half nervous half excited "Hi" back and handed over my visa and passport.

He looked at my passport, and then towards me. Then he again looked at my passport and said, "*Deshpande? Kuthle tumhi?*"

To say I was startled would be an understatement. Of all the questions I imagined that the immigration officer would ask, asking me "*Deshpande? Kuthle tumhi?*" (Deshpande? Which city are you from?) in Marathi was not on it at all.

"Aurangabad," I said with probably one of the biggest grins on my face.

"*Arewa! Magchya Diwali la amhi gelo hoto Aurangabad la. Ajintha-Ellora pahila.*" (Oh nice! We went to Aurangabad last Diwali. We saw Ajintha-Ellora caves).

I just could not believe the conversation I was having with my Immigration officer. "What's your name?" I asked.

"*Baher bhetla tar sangen. Ithe allowed nahi*" (If we meet outside I'll tell you, not allowed to disclose our identities here).

"Fair enough," I said.

He asked me about my course for a bit and that's it. I was officially into New Zealand!

What are the odds of my immigration officer in New Zealand being from the same country let alone the same state and with the same mother tongue as me who had gone on a family trip to my own city just a few months back!

But it wasn't all smooth sailing at the airport for me. Being a brown guy, and travelling alone at that, I was stopped for a "random security check" by a security officer just as I collected my luggage and was thinking whether to hail a cab right away or grab something to eat first.

He asked me for my ID. Then he asked me for my visa. Then asked which university I had enrolled in. Then asked about where I was going to stay.

I was so pissed off I even told him, "I know why you picked me for this random security check." In hindsight I probably shouldn't have said that. It was my first day in New Zealand. Did I really need to talk back to a security officer at the airport?

"I'm just doing my job," he said roughly, then proceeded to call my university, and my hostel to make sure the information I provided was correct. Only then I was allowed to go.

I went to the Vodafone store at the airport and bought a NZ SIM card. Then I walked outside of the airport building to hail a cab. It was raining. But not enough to justify putting your raincoat on. I got inside the cab, got comfortable. Then called my family back home.

I had my Indian accent moment in the cab when the cab driver asked me where to. My hostel was in a neighbourhood called Epsom (Ep-sum). Without actually finding out how it is pronounced, I had been blatantly mispronouncing it as 'Epsome'.

"Where to?" asked the driver.

"Epsome"

"I'm sorry where?"

"Rocklands hostel, Gillies Avenue, Epsom"

"Oh, you mean Epsum. Got it."

I couldn't let that random security check or the mispronunciation in the taxi get to me. I was in New Zealand! Yes it had been 48 hours since when I left my home in Aurangabad, and I was tired, jet lagged and maybe looked like a zombie. But I was in New Zealand. And that's all that mattered.

The hostel staff had already emailed me that as it was Saturday and they had a half-day off they might not be there to welcome me and show me around. So I had to collect my key from a little lockbox outside the hostel office, which had a digital lock, the pin of which they had shared over email.

My room was on the second floor of the building. And it was quite a task to take my 40 kilos of luggage up the stairs. The first thing that struck me about my hostel, and about New Zealand generally was how quiet it was. This was followed by the realisation of how clean it was. Followed by how green it was.

And this was Auckland- the financial capital where one third of the population lived. The Mumbai of New Zealand. If Auckland was so quiet and green and clean, I could not imagine how the little cities and towns would be. My friend lives in Tauranga. They call it a city but it is a really small town near Auckland. She often says it is so quiet there she has to check her pulse twice a day to make sure she's alive. I had my own taste of that experience when I went to live on Waiheke Island a couple of years later.

I don't remember what I had for lunch that day. But I do remember that I slept like a baby and only woke up at 2 a.m. to use the bathroom. I didn't have a bathroom in the room. We had common toilets and bathrooms, three of each on a floor with ten rooms.

My room door was one of those that automatically locks when closed. That wasn't a problem, as long as I carried my room key with me at all times. I think you already know where this is going. That night at 2 a.m. when nature's call woke me up, I not only forgot to carry my key but also my mobile, and as soon as I closed the door behind me, I knew I was fucked.

I panicked. Not even 24 hours in the country and I had messed up. I paced around the floor waiting for someone to show. But it was 2 a.m. The chances of that happening were next to nothing. Then I remembered there was a landline phone downstairs.

I went downstairs. But I didn't know whom to call. I didn't know the 911 of NZ. And the office was long closed. There was no one on the bottom floors too. I came back upstairs, answered the call of nature, and then began pacing up and down the corridor. I thought I might have to spend the night here in the corridor itself.

However, a few minutes later, an elderly gentleman stepped out from one of the rooms. He had just a towel wrapped around him and looked like he was about to go take a shower. He was as startled to see me as I was relived to see him. I told him about my situation. He had a look of suspicion on his face more than anything else. I asked him what is the 911 of NZ, he said 111. I asked can you please give me your cell phone so I could call them.

He hesitated for a bit. I don't know why. Then oh so reluctantly he opened the door of his room, grabbed his cell phone, which, by the looks of it, was the first edition of the first ever cell phone. I caught a glimpse of his room. There were so many books. The old man could have built a library of his own. And he looked like a wise, old, well-read man. Bald head, but hair everywhere else, and a full white beard.

I called 111.

A lady was on the other side.

"What is your emergency?" she asked.

I was embarrassed to tell her my "emergency." I'm just glad she didn't laugh.

"Wait for a few minutes, sir. One of our officers will be there. Don't worry." I could sense that she could sense that I was panicking. I thanked the old man and gave him his mobile phone back, and started my wait for the emergency services to arrive.

It didn't take long. Fifteen minutes later, there was a young man on my floor with a bunch of keys in his hand. I showed him to my room door, he tried a couple of keys, and, voila, it opened. Oh the relief. I thanked the gentleman and closed the door making a note to never leave again without my key and my cell phone. That one hour I was outside felt like a week.

Say Yes- Then Learn How to Do It

I didn't share this getting locked outside incident with family back home. I didn't want them to worry as it was my first time staying so far away from home. In hindsight it was more a funny incident than a scary one. The funnier part is the old man on my floor who helped me call '111', our rooms were facing each other. And after that I never saw him again. I lived in that hostel for seven months and that was the only time I saw him. I was glad I did though. I didn't even ask for his name. I don't think he even spoke a word apart from '111'. It was all gestures. He'd make a great actor. Like Pankaj Tripathi, whose neck does better acting than most.

The first thing I did on my first day in New Zealand was email the two most important people for me there: Mike Johnson (my mentor at the university) and Doug Cowie (Umpiring head at Auckland Cricket), and let them know I was there and asked for a time to meet.

Mike set up a meeting at his office at the University on the coming Tuesday. It was going to be kind of a ritual for us. And Doug invited me to their weekly umpire's meet at Eden Park on Monday evening. In the email he sent the four-digit security code to enter Eden Park. Eden Park isn't my favourite cricket ground. It's not even my favourite Auckland cricket ground. Yet, it is still a cricket ground, and part of the glorious history of cricket. It is where Sachin Tendulkar first opened the batting for India back in 1994. To say I was excited would be an understatement.

I just could not believe how nice and welcoming Doug was in his emails. This is a former international umpire we are talking about. And an active international cricket ground. If you don't know what I mean, try entering a cricket ground in India on non-match days. Any cricket ground. The security won't let you. They behave as if they are guarding a top-secret government project and no-one is allowed to see. You'll get a stick on your back if you peek. It is a tragedy how Indian cricket treats the fan, but that is a topic for another day.

My task for the day was to get some groceries, just milk and bread etc, and find out where the bus stop was and which bus would take me to Eden Park the next day. The grocery store was 500 metres from my hostel, and was run by an overly friendly Punjabi Indian uncle with a Kiwi-Punjabi accent. He also showed me the bus stop, which was just across the street from his shop. Looking at the schedule and maps of buses, I figured out which one would take me to Eden Park.

It was my second day in Auckland and my interactions so far were: Indian immigration officer at Auckland airport, Indian cab driver who took me to my hostel, and Indian grocery store owner. Everyone was quite helpful though. The rest of the day was spent in setting up my room and calling family and friends back home and taking pictures of the beautiful neighbourhood.

The big day arrived. I went to the bus stop fifteen minutes before my bus was supposed to come. It arrived right on time. I got in.

"Good evening! How are you doing?" said the driver with a huge smile on his face.

I was taken aback. I was not used to drivers greeting me while boarding a bus. I lived in India. If a driver greeted me that way while boarding, I would get off that bus right away. But in New Zealand as I soon learned it was a norm for bus drivers to greet passengers and vice versa. Even while getting off from the back door of the bus, I noticed most of the people shouted, "Thank you driver," and the driver gave them thumbs up in the mirror. *What a polite society* I might have thought. But actually I thought, *this is Monday evening. Most of these blokes have had a full day at work including the driver. If they have the energy to greet strangers at this time, does this mean these people are actually... happy?*

There are small red buttons near to every seat in the bus. You are supposed to push that red button when you get near to your stop, then a big sign lights up near the driver so he knows he has to stop there. The bus doesn't stop unless you push the button or there is someone getting on or off from the same stop. As it was my first bus ride, of course I didn't know that. When my stop arrived, I just got up and started walking towards the front as we do in India. My stop went by. The bus didn't stop. I was near the driver now.

"That was my stop," I said.

"Oh was it? Sorry maybe I didn't see the light go off," he said.

It was my mistake and the driver apologised. Once again I was perplexed. How happy were these people?

I got off and started walking towards Eden Park, a rugby venue, which is also used for cricket, as is the case with most grounds in NZ except Basin Reserve in Wellington and Hagley Oval in Christchurch to name a few. I'm a sucker for cricket grounds. The architecture, the grass, the history. I can spend hours just sitting in an empty cricket stadium. So, I was already bubbling with excitement and to my surprise, I wasn't nervous at all.

I walked to the gate. Entered the security code which Doug had sent in the email and then I was in. Our meetings were usually held in the Bert Sutcliffe lounge at the Eden Park outer oval. I got in, introduced myself to Doug who was very warm and welcoming. Then I went and sat somewhere at the back. I was just going to observe and take it all in.

The meeting began. It was their usual weekly meeting. The umpires who had just done the weekend games shared a few incidents. Doug made a few announcements. A few questions were asked and answered. Someone reminded Doug of that infamous Flintoff dismissal of his, which I later learned was a recurring theme. A few laughs echoed in the room.

Then Doug said, "Unfortunately, an umpire has backed out of this Saturday's women's 50 over match at Lloyd Elsmore Park so can someone please step in for him?"

I raised my hand. I do not know how and why I felt confident to volunteer myself to umpire a 50 over game when I had never umpired in my life before. And add to that I was in a different country, and didn't even know what the competition was or what the rules were at all. I was still jet lagged in fact. Yet I raised my hand. Doug looked surprised but impressed.

"Would you do it, Viraj?"

"Yes."

You know that famous Richard Branson quote: *If someone offers you an amazing opportunity but you don't know how to do it, say yes, then learn how to do it later.* This was my Richard Branson moment.

This was a professional game with a few players who had already represented New Zealand and few knocking the doors. I hadn't had a single lesson on umpiring. I did not even know the rules. Nor did I have any umpiring gear or kit. I do not know from where I got the confidence to say yes. Doug looked impressed.

At the end of the meeting, Doug made another announcement. He had two tickets for Next Saturday's New Zealand vs South Africa ODI at Eden Park to give away. "Who wants it," he asked.

A few hands rose.

I lifted my hand and said. "I deserve it as I'm the newest here.

The tickets were mine. I could not believe my luck.

After the meeting was over Doug sorted me out with the official umpiring shirt of Auckland Cricket and a huge kit bag that had everything an umpire could need. I walked in to Eden Park that day empty handed and walked out with the official Auckland Cricket umpiring kit, gear, tickets to NZ V SA ODI, and a potential umpiring debut the coming Saturday. I was grinning ear to ear.

In all that excitement and happiness, I failed to realize it was still kind of my first day in that country and I had forgotten to look for the bus back to hostel. And I had no clue which direction to go to look for a bus stop. It was also late. So I asked a fellow umpire. He showed me towards the main road. I walked to the bus stop there. The last bus had already gone. So I booked an Uber, and then got some Indian takeaway. What a day!

Are You 9/11 Brown or 7/11 Brown?

These last few days had taken every ounce of energy from my introvert self. But I had no time to rest. I had a meeting with my mentor, Mike Johnson, at his office in the university the next day. So late on Monday night after coming back to the hostel from Eden Park, I went over my notes for the meeting and also looked for buses I could take to and from the University.

The meeting was at 11 am. I took the 9:40 a.m. Outerlink bus to the university. It got me there at 10:30. A 10-minute walk later I was at the WT tower of the Auckland University of Technology. This is where the department of language and culture was. Mike's office, my classes everything was in that WT building. I bumped into Mike while walking into the tower. We exchanged pleasantries and I told him what a beautiful tower it was, and so high I almost sprained my neck looking up.

When I first talked with Mike on Skype and then did a Google search on him and saw his photos, I thought Dumbledore himself was going to mentor me. And when I met Mike, I was certain about it. Mike is a Dumbledore doppelganger if I've ever seen one. The hat. The white beard. That affable smile and personality. The age. The profession. Everything matches with Dumbledore. I wasn't Harry Potter by any means, not even close. But Mike was Dumbledore.

One of the first questions Mike asked me was if I was a Hindu or a Muslim. Maybe he wanted to know if I was a 7/11 brown or a 9/11 brown? In hindsight, maybe it hadn't been a good idea to compliment the tower earlier. A brown man who's just got off the airplane complimenting an iconic tower in your city centre. It must have set off a few alarm bells in the old white man's head. I said, "I'm a Hindu."

We sat in his office for around 40 minutes as Mike guided me through the course and what to expect from it. We had classes every Wednesday, and Mike said we'd meet every Tuesday either in his office or in one of the cafes in Auckland city where I would hand him over the work I'd done so far and go through his remarks on it.

Then Mike said, "let's go out and have coffee, my shout. In NZ whenever we want to treat someone, we say my shout."

We went downstairs and walked across the street to one of the coffee shops near the Aotea square.

"We really have lots of good coffee shops in Auckland, but this is one of my favourites," remarked Mike as we entered the café.

Mike ordered tea for himself and asked what would I have.

"black coffee," I said.

Mike laughed. The irony wasn't lost on him. Look at us he said. "The European drinking Chai tea and the Indian drinking coffee."

I had a huge urge to correct that, "Chai tea," but I didn't think correcting my mentor the day I met him was a very good idea. So, I held back and laughed and left the corrections part for later, and I did do it. But by this time, I had started addressing him as 'Mike' in my emails and not 'Sir.' So, our relationship was strong enough to handle the Chai tea conversation. In fact, it was so strong I also added the naan bread while we were at it, because why not?

He also asked about me, my family, my background etc. Then he asked about India and talked about when he went to India back in the early seventies. Mike then talked about his work outside of the university. His writings, his books, and his publishing house.

While talking about his publishing house he said, "Let me know what you think and I don't want you to feel any pressure to say yes just because I'm your mentor, but we (his publishing house) would like to publish your thesis as a non-fiction book."

I was not surprised at all. In fact, I kind of expected it. When I first heard that he was going to be my mentor, I did a Google search on the man, as you do, and I found out that he runs a publishing house. And my book was about Indian cricket post 2000 revolving around MS Dhoni's career. India is a huge market for publishers and cricket is the biggest thing in India. So, I took an educated guess that Mike would be interested in my thesis from a publishing point of view as well.

I told Mike I'd be honoured. But I kind of expected it, and how I had also told my mom that this would happen. We both laughed. Nothing could take the smile off my face that day. I was so new in this country that I still had a bit of jet lag. I had an umpiring debut, a potential book deal and tickets to a One Day International at Eden Park in my hand. I was flying!

Not Recognising a NZ Star Cricketer While Umpiring

My umpiring debut was getting closer each day, but I was yet to receive the official email from Doug. The email would contain information about the teams, the match, the venue, and most importantly, contact details of my umpiring colleague for the game. The email arrived on Thursday. The game was on Saturday.

The game was a Women's premier 50 over contest between Howick-Pakuranga Cricket Club and Cornwall Cricket Club. The venue was Lloyd Elsmore Park, pitch number 4. I had never heard of any of these terms before. The first thing I did was look up the venue on the map. It was 15 km away from my hostel and took one hour by bus. But by car it said only 18 minutes. So I decided to ask the fellow umpire, Geoff Young, if he could pick me up.

Geoff wasn't at the meeting at Eden Park, so I was yet to meet him. I decided to send him a long email the gist of it was: *Hi Geoff. I'm nervous. Please help.* Geoff was very helpful and sent a long reply, which calmed me down. First, he told me which rules I needed to study for the game, as a 50 over premier women's game in Auckland has a different set of rules than say a 50 over women's domestic game in India. He also offered to give me a ride to and from the game.

"Don't worry," he said, "the girls are easy to umpire. Some of them are so honest they even walk for Leg befores" (Leg before wicket is a form of dismissal in cricket). What? Surely Geoff was exaggerating to calm my nerves, I thought.

I started my preparation for the game. I looked up that ground and the matches played there this season. Looked at the scores. Then looked at the last five matches of the two teams. Looked at the common mode of dismissals. I concluded two things: not a high scoring ground, and straight balls get wickets.

The day arrived. Geoff Young arrived right on time. Pleasantries were exchanged, kit bags were put in the trunk and off we went. To my surprise, I wasn't as nervous as I thought I'd be. Maybe because Geoff's email had really calmed my nerves, or maybe because I had company in Geoff to guide me through the game, or maybe it was just the wonderful scenery outside which took my mind off the game. I remember telling Geoff a couple of times in the car how lucky they were to be living here in this paradise.

Llyod Elsmore Park is a huge playing field big enough to fit four cricket grounds. And on our match day, three of them were occupied. Ours was pitch no.4, the farthest one from the pavilion. So, we had to walk the longest to get to our ground. I was consciously observing Geoff and making mental notes for the games ahead. Tagging behind him as he went to speak with the captains, and the groundsman, and went to inspect the pitch, and the playing field. I was learning on the job.

I made one request to Geoff, to please take the first over and let me stand at square leg. He was fine with it. And soon, it was time. We went inside. As soon as we crossed the line all my jitters went away. They were replaced by a sense of belonging. A feeling of comfort even. I had been in this country for a week now and this was the first time I felt like I belonged there. I felt at home. Cricket was home. And the best part was I felt powerful. That umpiring shirt brought in a bit of authority and power as 22 people look up to you to make the decisions. And I loved that feeling of being in charge. Felt I was a few inches taller.

The first over went by without an event and it was my turn. My first over, which was the second over of the match was uneventful as well. I had to make my first decision in the eighth over of the match. A yorker hit the batter full on the toe, the bowler and her team went up in unison and just as I was raising my finger, the batter started walking! The batter walked for an LBW! Geoff wasn't kidding in the email. I collected the ball, went over to Geoff and we had a laugh about it. He had I told you so written all over his face. I was just happy I got my first decision right.

Plenty of action happened at my end that innings. I gave a leg before, caught behind, run out, and a stumping from square leg. The Cornwall Women made just 93 of which 31 were extras including 27 wides! The Howick women chased it down in 16 overs with 8 wickets in hand.

The game ended early, but I was drained. I was so focussed on getting the decisions right that I didn't switch off even between balls. I didn't talk to the non-striker or the fielder at square leg while standing there, which is something umpire's do to just switch off. I made a mental note of changing that next game.

Geoff asked if I'd have a beer as we entered the pavilion. Almost every cricket ground in NZ has a bar inside the club pavilion.

I was taken aback by this, and said, "Ok maybe one. I'm on a tight student budget."

"Don't worry," he said, "it's on the house. We get two beers after every game, on the house."

I could not believe it. Two cold beers on the house in the evening after standing in the field for over six hours on a hot summer's day? Heaven. That wasn't my only surprise for the evening. I looked around the club pavilion and saw New Zealand cricketer, Mitchell McClenaghan, sitting in his whites just twenty feet away.

There were three games of cricket happening at Llyod Elsmore Park that day and Mitchell was playing in one of them, making a comeback from an injury, trying to prove his fitness before he joined the Mumbai Indians for the upcoming IPL. The fan in me wanted to go say hi and take a pic. But the umpire in me thought it would be unprofessional. I went with the umpire.

I asked Geoff if he would like to join me at Eden Park next weekend for New Zealand v South Africa ODI. He said he'd love to and said he will pick me up and drop me off as well. So that was sorted. One more good thing happened post-game. The winning captain actually sought us umpires out and thanked us for our work.

Then she turned towards me and said, "My team and I came to know post-game that you're really new in the country and this is your first game. We all think you did a terrific job, and are glad to have a young umpire officiating our games. Usually, we just get old folks who can't even see properly like this one." She pointed at Geoff.

Laughter followed.

That was incredibly nice of her and once again I was left wondering, *how happy are these people exactly?*

Soon it was Tuesday, time for my second meeting with Mike. Now I knew which bus to take, which stop to get off at, everything. And I was still buzzing from the high of umpiring my first game, and the feedback I received from the captain. Mike congratulated me and said it is incredible that I managed to get a paying job this early.

I said I was surprised too. I had no formal training, prior experience and yet they gave me an umpiring debut and that too at a decent level game. Mike said it is the New Zealand way. We like to throw people in the deep end and see if they sink or swim. I think I managed to swim all right.

I sent a long email to Doug thanking him for the opportunity and shared my wonderful experience. I requested him to give me as many games as possible as the cricket season in New Zealand is only from October to March, so we were almost in the last month. Doug reciprocated by giving me nine games in March. I could only officiate in five of those due to university commitments.

But all those games were of different formats, with different colleagues, different age groups, different competitions, and of course different grounds. I got to travel all around Auckland and get a first-hand taste of the cricket there in my first month.

Doug made it a point to partner the new umpires with experienced ones. It meant there was always at least one experienced umpire at the ground in case any incident happens, and second, the new umpires get to learn a lot. I was a sponge for that one month, soaking up every bit of information.

My second game was with international umpire, Diana Venter, who had just officiated in the ICC T20 World Cup the year before. Diana was originally from South Africa but had been living and working in Auckland for past few years. She used to ride a sports bike to the cricket! On our match day though, she came to pick me up in a car. It was thoughtful of her. Because carrying both of our kit bags on a sports bike would have been a nightmare. And Auckland weather isn't suitable for bike rides at all.

Diana was so thorough and methodical in her work. It was like watching the ICC Umpire's Manual in action. I was watching her and she was watching me during the game. I, of course, in a hope to pick up something and she to see if she can correct a few things, which she did.

The first thing she corrected was the way I signalled four. At the end of my four signals my hand used to finish away from the body. She pointed out that it might seem like a no-ball to the scorer watching from afar. So suggested me to finish my hand movements closer to the body. And then gave me thumbs up from square leg when I signalled the four that way in the next over.

When the match was over, we had a couple of cold ones at the club while getting to know more about each other. It was more of me asking questions about ICC and about international cricket, and she patiently answering everything.

As we were about to leave, she asked me to stand on the balcony of the club with my back to the ground. She was going to take a picture of me in my umpiring gear at the end of a long hard-working day in the sun. I then took a few selfies with her as well. It was after all my first time umpiring with an international umpire.

Another interesting incident happened during that game at Colin Maiden Park. An Auckland University bowler handed me her cap and I asked her what her name was. To those unaware, it is a routine practice for umpires to ask bowlers their names so we can keep a track on how many overs they've bowled on our little notepad.

The only problem was the bowler in question who had handed me her cap was Anna Peterson. A New Zealand international who had just taken a hat-trick against Australia last month. She looked taken aback but just for a second, and then ala James Bond, she said, "Peterson... Anna Peterson."

I didn't remember how Anna Peterson looked but I was surely familiar with the name thanks to her being in the news very recently. The realization was fast coming over me. *It's her isn't it*, was all my mind could think.

During the drinks break I confirmed the same with Diana. "She's Anna Peterson the same girl who took a hat-trick the other day right?"

"Yes," said Diana.

Oh dear Lord. In only my second game of my umpiring career I had asked a current New Zealand star cricketer what her name was! Much to my relief Anna was pretty chilled about it. While shaking hands post-game I did apologize for not recognising her and congratulated her on her hat-trick.

"Don't worry about it, mate, happens," she said with a smile.

Not everything was hunky dory. There were a few unpleasant incidents as well. During a tournament semi-final where I was again officiating with Geoff, a really unpleasant incident happened. I was standing at square leg. Geoff was the main umpire. There was a huge appeal for caught behind. Geoff paused for a bit and then started walking towards me. He was yet to make a decision.

Seeing him come my way I walked towards him. We met at mid-wicket where he asked me did I hear a nick, I said I heard something but I'm not sure it was bat. He said he heard a loud nick and he was pretty confident it was bat and just wanted to confirm with me. Being at square leg I wasn't in the best position to see a nick outside off stump. So I told him to go with his gut. Which he did and gave the batsman out.

There were a few moans and boos from the dressing rooms. But when you're in the middle you don't focus on that, there is too much going on already.

When the game finished, while shaking hands with the teams, one coach said to me in a sarcastic tone: "Good job, first time I saw square leg give caught behind."

"Hold up," I said, "Square leg didn't give any caught behind. You weren't in the middle you don't know what happened."

But he was dismissive and disrespectful. I felt upset. But I couldn't vent my anger there on the ground. I was really new and it would have been unprofessional. So, I just vented it out in an email to Doug, who was supportive and said this was not the first complaint he had received about that particular coach and told me I did the right thing.

Next morning, after having slept over it, I played the incident in my mind from that coach's perspective. There is an appeal for caught behind, the umpire doesn't give it out but walks towards the square leg umpire, they have a conversation and then the umpire gives it out. So, it was understandable how he thought I was the one who convinced Geoff to raise his finger. When in fact I had told Geoff, I was unsure whether he nicked it or not. Geoff went with his gut.

But he did so only after consulting with me, which made me the villain in the coach's book. Not sure if I could have done anything different there. And I would have been sympathetic to the coach, if not for his disrespectful behaviour. One thing was sure. I needed to have a really thick skin if I wanted to become a good umpire.

Because there is pressure and you are going to make the odd wrong decision. If that decision goes in favour of the bowling team, the non-striker is in your ear immediately after and for quite a bit of time. If it happened to be in favour of the batting side the whole fielding team is now sledging you too along with the batsmen. You have to ignore all that and focus on the next ball.

Umpires are the eternal punching bag in cricket. For fans, for players, and for coaches. No one wants to accept they played poor cricket, they just want an excuse, a punching bag and that's where we come in. Umpires, selectors, and wicket keepers, these three in cricket are only noticed when they do something wrong, drop a catch, or give a bad decision or pick a bad team. TV channels and broadcasters make a whole package of bad decisions and dropped catches but will rarely do the same for good decisions. It is indeed a thankless job.

The song "Umpire" by the Irish pop band and the following lyrics in particular captures the situation perfectly:

Who would aspire to be an umpire and who would be a referee?
We're only here to be sneered at, just a relic of yesteryear
There was a time when we were held high, but it's not how it used to be
They only let us stick around so they've someone to kick around
One more relic of yesterday

The Audacity of the Caucasity

By now I had gotten comfortable with my routine. On weekdays I had classes and meetings with Mike, and on all weekends and some weekdays too I had games to umpire. The rest of the time was divided into writing my thesis and working on my website. As I was already earning a decent amount of revenue from my website, I had decided to continue working on it in NZ rather than taking a part time job. Add daily chores to it and the time was flying by.

I was the only Indian and also Asian kid in my class, which was quite a surprise to me considering the vast numbers of Indian and Asian students living there. We had twelve students in the class, I was among the youngest. Of those twelve students there were three girls named Elizabeth. An American girl and I were the only overseas students. It wasn't a diverse class at all, but it was exactly what I had signed up for.

On our first day of classes, we had the introductions and when my introduction was done, a fellow student let's call her 'Karen' said "Oh! You are from India?! I show my students Slumdog Millionaire every year."

Karen was in her forties, she was a teacher at a school in Auckland, and she said those words with an expression of superiority in her tone and on her face. I shouldn't have engaged. I should have just nodded and given a polite smile as I would have done if not for an unpleasant experience the day before.

The day before had been my first day at the university. I had missed the induction as my visa approval got delayed and I had to reschedule the flight. It was a whole thing. But the university had put these volunteers on campus for the first week or so to guide new students around campus, show what's where and that helped.

I asked one of the volunteers where the department of Language and Culture was. It was a bit far, on a different street actually. You had to cross a road and walk about 500 meters to get there from the main AUT building. She said she'll walk me there. *How nice of her*, I thought. We got to talking on our way there, just small talk. She asked me what I was going to study there and what the topic of my thesis was and where I was from. When I told her I was from India, she said "Oh India! One of my friends went there last year and she was like oh my God they have curries at McDonalds and I was like that's crazy, oh my God".

Now there is so much wrong in that statement. But the thing that annoyed me most was her superficial accent and the self-important tacky tone. But of course I didn't say anything back, I just half-smiled. But when the next day Karen brought up the topic of Slumdog Millionaire, I wasn't going to stay quiet.

"I haven't seen Slumdog Millionaire," I said.

"You haven't?" Karen was shocked to say the least.

"Slumdog Millionaire isn't a film about India. It is a film about the perception of India in Western countries. And that is the main reason why it did more business overseas than it did in India. It may have been a film about India but the target audience wasn't Indian people. And it achieved its goal."

"But it is a great film. I show it to my students every year""

"You're part of the problem then, Karen. Why would you show any piece of art or film or documentary to students that shows only one side of the story? Just because it reaffirms your beliefs? If I made a film about NZ and showed all the bad aspects of NZ would you want me to show it to every new generation of Indian kids? Corrupt their minds about New Zealand even before they'd got the ability to think and make their own decisions?" I was fuming. All the pent-up anger I had accumulated from my short stay in New Zealand so far had found the perfect outlet, and I let it all go.

"Oh I didn't know that" is all she said. Not even sorry, let alone the promise of showing her new batch of students something different. For all I know she's still showing Slumdog Millionaire to every new batch of kids at her school.

Imagine being a kid at that school. Imagine being an Indian kid at that school who was born in New Zealand. Imagine being a kid in Karen's class born in India but moved to New Zealand recently. Would the other kids not make fun of your country? Not make fun of you? Kids are kids, right? Even if no one makes fun of the Indian kid in the class, just imagine being that kid for a minute. How uncomfortable would you feel? How ashamed would you feel? Wouldn't it sow seeds of being inferior to your fellow batch mates in you just because you belong to a certain country? Media plays a huge part in this. In creating perception which at times is so far away from reality it's almost chalk and cheese. But media is the mirror to society, right? So, it is not solely to blame. Media shows what people want to see.

But comments like this, however banal, were not the only thing getting to me. Auckland runs a really good bus service. I must have taken hundreds of buses in my stay there. The buses are clean. They run on time. The drivers are polite. Everything is good. Some buses also have these digital screens that display headlines from around the world. In all the time I was in New Zealand and took local buses only once did I come across news about my homeland.

Headline: Indian pitch doctors take their craft to a new low in Ranchi.

Description: Australia's worst fears for the third Test have been realised, with India rubber-stamping a pitch stitch-up for the ages in Ranchi.

I was on my way to university. I had an important meeting with Mike, but my blood was boiling. This is what the media does, especially western media. They create these narratives. India doctor pitches at home to turn square as they can only win on turning pitches was their favourite narrative, until India beat Australia in Australia on fast bouncy pitches in back-to-back tours in 2018-19 and 2020-21.

For all that hue and cry about that pitch in Ranchi, the Test ended in a boring draw as Australia made 451 and India responded with 600. But just because the pitch was of a certain colour and it didn't sit well with the Australian media they termed it as pitch doctoring and that before even before a ball had been bowled. That draw felt as good as a win for India.

I was angry and disappointed to see that news on my bus to university in Auckland. New Zealand wasn't even playing that series for God's sake! But all these things piled up. That incident at the university with the volunteer, then the Slumdog Millionaire incident in class, and this bus incident, all of it stayed with me. I don't feel bad for my little outburst in class. It was needed. And that was the perfect audience. It was my Akshay Kumar in Namastay London moment or Shashi Tharoor at Oxford, if you will.

The sad part about this thing is it works both ways. Most of the Western World looks down on us and most of us in turn look up to them. I think we as a society, and by 'we', I mean India, are still suffering from the colonial hangover. It is there deep within us. It can be seen on the thousands of billboards for fairness creams. So deep is the notion of western superiority that we not only crave it, we go extra miles for it.

There is a massive colonial hangover in cricket. I'll talk about cricket because it is my area of interest but I'm sure there are numerous such examples in every walk of life. As cricket fans you might have come across content where the overseas cricketer talks something about Indian cricket and it becomes headline.

I understand if India are playing Australia and Mathew Hayden says something about India's openers then it understandable for it to become news. But India might be playing West Indies and you'll have Brad Hogg tweeting about the technique of Indian openers and that'll make it to sports pages across newspapers in the country. It is Brad Hogg. He is a spinner, and an Australian whose team isn't even playing the series. Yet, just because of the colonial hangover still present within our media and society that statement from Brad Hogg will get more press coverage than it should.

To give you some perspective it is like a statement from Amit Mishra about the defensive technique of David Warner during The Ashes making news in Australia. It is ridiculous. Leave poor Amit Mishra alone, have you ever seen Australian or English journalist seek the opinion of legends like Gavaskar, Tendulkar or Dravid about their team when India isn't playing them? Never.

Just look at the IPL for example. How many overseas coaches do you see in the IPL? Barring one or two franchises, every franchise has overseas coaching staff, and third-rate Aussie players are bought for enormous amounts of money just because of where they're from. It has changed a bit in recent years, but it's still quite prevalent. We as a society are hungry for validation especially from foreigners. That hunger is so huge that westerners reacting to Indian content has become one of the most watched genres on YouTube.

How Shashi Tharoor Helped Me Get Free Drinks in NZ

In my second week in NZ, Rocklands had organised a get together for all the new students and hostel residents to get to know each other. The get together was called "Sausage Sizzle." Yep, I kid you not. When the flyer about the event was slid under my door, I thought it was a flyer for a gay bar.

I was yet to make good friends there. And what's hostel life without a group of friends, so I wasn't going to let this sausage sizzle go to waste. Determined to make some friends, and eat some free food of course, I went to the sausage sizzle.

The first people I met were two German dudes, Niklas and Tristan. I knew they were German before they told me where they were from because their S's were Z's and W's were V's and vice-versa. They figured I was from India before I could say so as well. They were in Auckland for six months on a semester abroad program.

Then there was this real quiet and introverted guy, Cedrik from France. He was in Auckland to learn English. I don't know if it was the language barrier or his introvert nature but he didn't speak much. But what little he did was endearing because of the French accent. It's quite an unfair advantage that French accent.

Then there was Irham from Indonesia. He had a bit about him, and had a funky dressing style. He was there to learn fashion. He was quite an interesting personality and a fun guy to hang out with. When we met, the first thing he said was, "Thank God there is at least one person in this hostel who can pronounce my name right!"

There was someone else whose name people found difficult to pronounce. So much so that he had made up another easy to say mainstream name as a replacement for his original name. It is a common thing brown and black people do in majority white societies, make up a name that is easy for the white folks to pronounce. This guy was from Zimbabwe. While introducing himself he said his name was Daniel and he was from Zimbabwe.

After a few minutes when it was just me and him talking, I asked, "Mate, is your name really Daniel?"

"What do you mean?"

"I have a hunch that Daniel is your NZ name"

He laughed and said "Nkosi. Nkosi is my real name."

"Alright. I'm not going to call you Daniel, I'm going to call you Nkosi."

He had the biggest smile. Few weeks later everyone in the group was calling him Nkosi.

Our group was majority European. Apart from Niklas and Tristan, there was another German girl, Chiara. And couple of Dutch guys Benno and Stan. There was a girl from Belgium called Lein, but she never hung out with us much. The heart of our group was a guy from Singapore, Winston. Winston was doing his PhD. And he had been in the hostel longer than anyone else and he used to say, "I'm going to be the last man standing at the hostel from our group. He was still there last I checked."

I wasn't in the best shape in my first couple of months. Eating junk and not working out wasn't helping at all. But I didn't realise how unfit I was till I decided to join Stan, Niklas, and Tristan on their trek to One Tree Hill.

"How long is the walk?" I asked.

"About 45 minutes," said Stan.

"I can walk 45 minutes," I said and off we went.

What I did not know that it was 45 minutes one way for tall and fit people like those I was with. All three of them were taller and fitter than me. Tristan and Niklas used to walk an hour to the university, Stan would ride his bike. Whereas I took the bus.

It took us two hours to finish our little trek, thanks to me huffing and puffing and always asking them to wait for me. This was one of the first times we hung out and I think I made a pretty bad impression fitness wise, but we had a good time with lots of laughs, mostly at my expense.

The trek worked as a wakeup call and I started working out from the next day onwards. Well not technically the next day as my body was still sore from the trek but I started soon. There was a gym available in the hostel, and Niklas used to spend a lot of time there, but I wasn't a big fan of working out in a gym, preferring cardio workouts like skipping, jogging and even planks rather than sitting on a machine and lifting weights. So I started with that.

For the next few weeks, I did planks in my room and went to Melville Park near the hostel for a jog. Melville Park is beautiful and also hosts cricket and rugby matches. It is huge. I used to walk there which is around one kilometres one way. I would then run a couple of laps of the park then walk back.

If this wasn't a book and was in fact a movie, around this time, you'd be seeing a montage of me working out with eye of the tiger playing in the background, building up to my eventual redemption which in fact happened very soon at a place called Spitting Feathers.

We were students living on a budget, always on the lookout for a cheap meal or drink. We found our spots for both pretty early thanks to Stan who suggested a place called "Spitting Feathers" in downtown Auckland. Spitting Feathers was not the most happening place in

Auckland. It wasn't very popular either. And it was kind of hidden. It was close to the University and I had walked a bit around the Auckland city centre with friends, and I certainly remember walking the street Spitting Feathers was on, yet didn't see it till Stan took us there.

The best part about that place was that they served the cheapest booze in Auckland- $3 Heineken every Thursday. And that's all that mattered to us at that time. On our first visit to Spitting Feathers, I challenged Niklas to a plank off much to the laughter of everyone. I think there were eight of us and all were betting on Niklas. I don't remember if we actually took bets, the memory of that night isn't great. But I do remember me and Niklas doing a plank off right in the middle of a busy Auckland club. For the first few seconds I could hear our friends laugh at the stupidity of our act. Then the crowd joined in. Around 40 seconds in everyone there was glued to our little plank off. A few more seconds passed.

"I'm going to give up" Niklas said as I looked over to him. Any second now Niklas was going to fall and I was going to rise to the applause of the Spitting Feathers crowd.

At that very moment I felt a tap on my back. It was the club bouncer asking us to stop. I don't know why. If anything the place lit up due to our little plank off. Those bouncers came as a blessing to Niklas who had almost given up. To be fair to him, he acknowledged he was done and would have lost had the bouncers not intervened. Stan and Tristan who were there on that trek where I huffed and puffed my way and slowed everyone down told me they were impressed. No one thought the unfit Indian dude would beat the strong German guy who basically lived at the gym. Boy I was smug that night.

The last bus from the city to our hostel was at eleven. Yes, Auckland sleeps early. Despite being the financial capital and the most populous city in New Zealand, Auckland has some small town qualities, which I would put in the cons bracket rather than the pros bracket. The shops tend to be closed by 5 pm. Yes, you read that right. Imagine shops closing at 5pm in Mumbai. There are a few shops on busy Queen Street which are open till late but even they usually close at 8 pm.

When we left Spitting Feathers it was already past eleven, so we decided to eat something first and then Uber back to Rocklands. We never ate at Spitting Feathers, it was too costly. In fact, we never went to Spitting Feathers on a non-Thursday. That's how cheap we were.

Nkosi was going on and on about this place he had chicken from the other night. "It's better than KFC bro, I'm telling you." It was close by so we decided to give it a try. It was a small takeaway shop on Queen Street called 'Avachi'. There were a few chairs to sit on but it was mostly a takeaway shop. Nkosi suggested we try the thigh and the drum. So we did. For the next few minutes no one spoke anything. For the next hour or so all we spoke about was how good that chicken was.

It became a ritual. Every Thursday we went to Spitting Feathers for that $3 Heineken and then to Avachi for the chicken. Thirsty Thursday we called it. Some Thursdays there were ten of us, some Thursdays just four or five, but we went every Thursday. I don't think I ever missed a Thursday. I anyways didn't use to go out much. Cricket season had ended; I had classes only once a week. There were some weeks the meeting with Mike was held online so I was cooped up in my room most of the time. Also going out meant spending money so I used to minimize going out as much as possible, just Thursdays I would say.

And every Thursday something would happen that would make it a memorable night. One of my favourite Thirsty Thursdays was when Shashi Tharoor helped us get free beer. Yep, not kidding. This one Thursday on a cold winter night it was just the three of us that went out. Myself, Irham and Benno. One of Benno's work mates was going to join us there, Matt from England. So an Indian guy, an Indonesian guy, a Dutch guy and a British guy walked into a bar. Guess what they talked about? Colonization!

At first I didn't see the irony of it all as I didn't know the Netherlands had colonised Indonesia for 200 years! It was when Benno said that he went to Indonesia on a family trip last year as they have a lot of Dutch history there that I became intrigued.

"What do you mean you have history there?" I asked

"Netherlands ruled us for 200 years, brother. I'm surprised you didn't know!" said Irham before Benno could answer.

"What the fuck, man! You let this little nation rule you for 200 years!" I was shocked both about my lack of knowledge and about what my lack of knowledge was about.

"Well hold up, bro," said Irham, who then pointed to Matt."Didn't these guys rule you for over a 100 years too?! So dear, pot, please don't call the kettle black, you know."

At that moment mine and Irham's connection went to a different level. Joined by the suffering of our ancestors due to Western colonization and the mutual hatred for what the ancestors of the two guys sitting with us had caused us formed an unbreakable bond as we talked about the atrocities that took place in our countries.

Looking at us talk about the bad things their countries had done Benno and Matt were shocked. They couldn't believe what we were talking about because you see history is written by the conqueror. The history they were taught in school was completely different from the history we were taught.

Before we knew it, our casual Thursday night out became a full-fledged discussion on colonization and reparation. Me and Irham shared dreadful incidents that happened in our countries during that time we could see the body language change of both Matt and Benno move from disbelief to sadness, then from sadness to guilt, as I showed them that famous Shashi Tharoor speech at Oxford University.

The guilt was so heavy they decided to pay for everything that night. "Least we can do" Benno said. And that's how Shahi Tharoor helped me get free drinks in New Zealand.

What Happens When You Make Masala Chai in a Mostly White Hostel

I'm a morning person, but at Rocklands I used to wake up late. By late I mean 8.30 a.m. You see when you live in a hostel and have to share toilets and bathrooms with other people you have to figure out ways to use the toilet and bathroom so firstly there is no waiting and secondly it is clean.

The workday starts early in New Zealand. Most offices are open before nine. So there were a lot more people using the toilets and bathrooms between 6-8 than they were between 8-10. Also there was a cleaning lady who used to come every morning at 8. So I would usually wake up at 8 so I could get to use the clean bathrooms without having to wait for anyone to finish.

The cleaner was an old blonde lady called Eve. After the first few days of exchanging pleasantries, I told her what a great job she does and this feels like a hotel and not a hostel thanks to her.

"You're very kind, young man," she said, smiling from ear to ear.

My hostel wasn't a student hostel. It was shared accommodation for everyone. So there were people of all age groups living there, even quite a few retired people. One such gentleman was Otto from the Czech Republic.

Otto lived on the same floor as me, and our routines were similar. So almost every day we would bump into each other at the bathrooms or the kitchen. Otto loved a chat. He was very inquisitive and a very good listener. He was the same age as my grandfather, around 75 at that time. And we got along really well.

He had seen it all. He had travelled all over the world, lived in multiple countries. Done different jobs. In Auckland he used to run a courier business. He had climbed the Himalayas a few times, and even been to Antarctica a couple of times too. I was surprised by his knowledge about India, and also cricket. He loved India.

I went to New Zealand in early 2017. Demonetisation, where the government had voided the validity of certain bank-notes, resulting cash shortages had just occurred and was a hot topic in India. So obviously it was the first thing I told Otto when he asked, "what's going on in India at the moment." He couldn't believe it. I think that was the first conversation we had.

Otto had a distinct style of speaking. He used to repeat every other sentence three times. He became my sounding board, my go to man, my agony uncle if you like. I loved chatting with him. And he loved chatting too.

"I've seen many young people live here," he once said. "But all of them ignore the old folks. They only talk with other young people. You are the exception." Those words stayed with me for a long time.

I think Otto was the most affected when I left the hostel. He used to literally count the days. *Ten days to go before you go back, nine days to go...* and so on. What he exactly used to say was, "Ten days to go before you before you before you go back, eh?" Saying certain words three times was the Otto trademark.

A day before I left, we met in the kitchen as usual, just like every day for the past six-seven months. I could see Otto was taking it a bit harder than I'd anticipated. His eyes were watery. I felt bad for him.

I knew the feeling. I had felt a similar way when my other hostel mates left. That's why when I went back to New Zealand later, even though I wasn't living at Rockland's, I made it a point to go there just to surprise Otto. And I got a friend to record the moment. Otto was delighted.

Rocklands is a big hostel, part of it built in that grand wooden colonial style, with four different building offering different type of accommodation, women only, unisex, ensuite etc. And it has a huge kitchen and common area, gym and more at one end of the place. My building and especially my room was the furthest from the main kitchen. There was also a small kitchenette in my building on the second floor but it only had a microwave and a toaster. I couldn't make tea there.

So every afternoon around 4 p.m. I used to go the main kitchen to make tea. Proper *desi adrak wali kadak chai* (Proper Indian masala tea). You know how aroma spreads when you're making tea. Even your neighbours know that tea is being prepared. The kitchen was open plan adjacent to the large common room. When I first made tea there, I was the only one in the kitchen. As the tea started to boil a few people came in from the common room, following the smell, I guess.

One of them was Winston. "What are you cooking that smells so great?" he asked

"It's just tea, brother." I said.

He could not believe it. "I've been having tea my whole life and it never smelled so good," he said.

After the tea was made, I handed him a cup. He loved it so much he asked me for the recipe and also asked which tea powder it was. Then bought it the next day from an Indian store nearby!

Seeing how much he loved the tea, I decided to take the boys to eat some Indian chaat. We had pani puri, dahi puri, and samosa. It was too spicy for the Europeans, but Winston and Irham loved it. They loved it so much we went there often, and even when I was back in

India, they used to go there and send me pics.

Rocklands was not the only place I lived in New Zealand. I lived with a Kiwi family at a suburb near the beach. I lived on my own in a small cabin on Waiheke Island. I also lived in a dorm, sharing a huge room with seven other people from all over the world. All of this was part my plan to fully experience and immerse myself in the culture and get as much as possible out of my time here.

Food really helped me along the way. Tea became my signature. Wherever I lived, on my first day I made tea for everyone and as usual tea was followed by talks and more tea. It helped me connect with people and make new friends, be it in a different hostel or my first homestay.

My first homestay host was Judy. I wasn't supposed to live with Judy. I was supposed to live with her aunty, Sue, having booked her homestay. However, two days before my flight to New Zealand, Sue called and said she wouldn't be able to host me as she was unwell, but she'd made arrangements for me to stay at her niece's place.

"Okay," I said, well to be honest, I had no other options. Few moments later her niece called. She was a single mum of three girls of which two had already left home. She lived in Beachaven and had a dog. Beachaven is exactly like it sounds, a haven surrounded by beaches.

"Where's the nearest beach?" was my first question to Judy when I got there.

"Walk 10 minutes in any direction" she said and laughed, following it up with, "We can go there in the evening." My first day at Judy's place was pretty eventful.

First, we went to visit her uncle who lived nearby in a facility for old people. We gave him some medicines and checked how he was doing. Then we picked up Stephanie, Judy's twelve-year-old daughter from school.

In the car Judy asked if I could pay this week's rent that day.

"Sure," I said, "but we need to run to the ATM first."

"Yay now we can buy some stuff, Steph," she said. It was then I realised what a tight spot she was in financially.

Unfortunately, I couldn't remember my ATM pin and my card got blocked so we had to go to the bank and request a new card, withdraw the required cash and then do some grocery shopping.

On our way back we went to the beach. Judy's dog, Piggles, was in the car and we all had a great time at the beach playing fetch with Piggles. There was a boat anchored near the beach. I asked Judy about it. She told me it belonged to a guy called John. John lived on the boat. When he was hungry or needed to use the toilet, he would come ashore do his business and then go back. "He's weird," she said, "kind of a loner."

A short while later John came by. Judy greeted him and introduced me.

"Hi John," I said.

He went completely nuts. "You fucking go back to your own country, fuckers come here and take our jobs. We don't need you."

Aside from being a loner, John also turned out to be racist. I wanted to give it back to him, but Judy stopped me. "He knows where I live. God knows what he's capable of, leave it." That incident cast a cold shadow on what had been a great first day at my new Beachaven home.

Small Cappuccino Three and a Half Sugars

One of the perks of being an Auckland cricket Umpire is you get tickets for the international games. During the summer of 2019-20 India were in New Zealand, with two T20Is scheduled at Eden Park. The first was on the twenty-fourth of January and second on the twenty-sixth. I went to the first game, watched India smash NZ to pieces, then I umpired for 90 overs on the twenty-fifth. As I was tired and had already watched the first T20I I thought of selling the ticket for the second game on Facebook. I Got quite a few responses, finalised a deal with a guy who was going to pick the ticket up on the match day afternoon.

But on the match day morning, I had a change of heart. It just didn't feel right to sell the ticket. And I had a real gut feeling that something magical was going to happen that night and I didn't want to miss it. My gut is usually reliable when it comes to cricket, but not this time as far as the game was concerned. It was a snoozefest. New Zealand made a below par score which India chased down without a sweat. I don't remember a single ball, shot, catch, or anything from the game.

However, something memorable did happen. There was a big group of Kiwi fans in the row behind me and we were bantering back and forth throughout, when during the second innings, I realised that the gentleman sitting one seat from me was former New Zealand captain Daniel Vettori! I wasn't 100% sure and I needed confirmation, so I asked the Kiwi lads who I was bantering with if they also thought he was Dan Vettori. To my surprise they did that 'Yeah nah' thing which Kiwis do to disagree with someone but to soften the blow with an affirmative yeah first.

So naturally we had a bet. Loser to buy the next round. It was in fact Dan the man himself. And your boy got free drinks. Dan was on national TV last evening during a rugby event and he had a full beard, which he shaved this morning. And that's the reason your boy won the bet. So, the lesson is, if you want to win bets at the cricket don't watch rugby on TV.

The Indian fans were having a party outside Eden Park after the game with people dancing to the beats of dhols while patriotic Indian songs played. Naturally I joined the party, and repeated the only two dance steps I know as many times as I could before reluctantly dragging myself to the train station.

Auckland Transport gets its share of flack and deservedly so, however one good thing they do is make the trains free from Eden Park to the city on every match day, be it cricket or rugby. And it is a life saver. I mean it in the most literal sense. Because people don't go to watch sporting events at Eden Park, they go to get drunk with their mates and chat shit while the game happens in the background. And you don't want those blokes behind the wheel.

I got off at Britomart train station and while walking towards the escalator I noticed a beautiful girl walking with her friend. So as any straight male or lesbian female would, I increased my pace so I could get a closer look. And by sheer coincidence and nothing else I happened to be behind them when it was time to step on to the escalator. Lo behold, that beautiful girl was speaking in my mother tongue with her friend!

"Excuse me, are you Maharashtrian?"

"Umm yes"

"*Oh me pan.* I'm Viraj" (Oh me too)

"Hi, *me Parvati, ani hee Shewta*" (I'm Parvati, and this is Shweta)

So, we started talking as we walked out of the station. There's a McDonalds right next to the train station.

"Would you like to get some ice cream," I asked. Because no sane person ever says no to an ice cream, especially not a free one. As it turns out, they were sane.

Then we walked right to the edge of the harbour and found a nice spot to put our feet up and continue the conversation. We must have spent an hour there just talking and laughing. It didn't feel like we'd met just a couple of hours ago. When we started walking back, I of course didn't want the night to end and suggested we get some coffee. Shweta wasn't up for it but Parvati was and we started walking around the Auckland CBD in search of a place that could serve us coffee at 2 am.

We found a place that had coffee. I got a long black. Shweta still hadn't changed her mind so she didn't get anything, but Parvati got a small cappuccino with three and a half sugars! Now I love my coffee. My day doesn't start without it. I have my coffee as God intended it to be consumed. Hot, black, no milk, no sugar. However, I do understand that everyone is not the same and one should have an open mind and respect each other's different choices.

And I do respect other people's coffee choices as long as their coffee can be ordered using two words or less. Don't get me wrong, people who take their coffee black like me are no saints, quite the opposite in fact according to the study published in Indian PM Narendra Modi's good friend 'Doland' Trump's 'Covfefe' university, people who take their coffee black are more likely to exhibit psychotic traits. And the people who order a Venti iced hazelnut macchiato sugar syrup extra caramel extra shot light ice are their most likely victims.

So when Parvati asked for three and a half sugars in her small cappuccino my body inadvertently took a step away from her. It was as if my whole body said, "brother ew."

"What! I always take three and a half sugar in my cappuccino."

I was too stunned to speak. I could see the shock and disbelief paired with sadness in the cafe man's eyes. I had no doubt that while my mind was going, "ew, brother ew, what's that!" His mind was going "look how they massacred my boy!"

The coffee was alright. But it was never about the coffee anyway. It was about stretching that night out as long as we could. We were drinking our coffee on a bench on Queen Street at 3 a.m. as you do, when four drunk guys walked up to us.

Shweta and I were sitting on the two ends of the bench with Parvati between us. The bench was big enough to sit four people. One of the guys sat next to Shweta and put his arm around her. And without thinking I got up, sat in between the two of them and put my arm around that guy.

"Cut it," I said.

I didn't know what got into me. Maybe I wanted to be a hero to impress the girls I had just met. Thankfully the guys walked off cos I did not have any plan B, and had they not backed down, the situation could have ended in me getting badly beaten up.

If the girls weren't with me and had a similar incident happened, I would never have gotten involved. Four vs one, are you kidding me? I had no chance. This wasn't a Bollywood movie. Real life unfortunately has things like logic and the consequences of your actions that we always have to keep in mind.

The only logical option I would have had, would be to run towards my hostel which was about a 100 meters away from there and I'm a surprisingly good sprinter. I love a sprint and I'm always up for a race. I once challenged Nkosi to a sprint to the bus stop on one of our night outs, and beat him. Then, as no one would believe that a non-athletic Indian dude beat a tall fit-as-a-fiddle African male made specifically to win races all around the world but forced to start a family, go out for milk and never come back, I recorded a video post of our race saying things like, *I'm the new Usain Bolt*. Every time that video is played one of Nkosi's ancestors turns in their grave.

The silver lining of the incident with drunk guys was that it gave me the perfect excuse to walk the girls home. They lived in the same apartment building (different flats) about one and a half kilometres away. While crossing the road near her home I held Parvati's hand. Parvati would later tell me that that was the first moment she felt something. She said, "It was like electric shockwaves throughout my body, and I couldn't figure out why or what was happening!"

It was around 3:30 a.m. when we reached their place. We clicked a few selfies and then as I was about to take their leave, Parvati asked would I like to come up for a varan bhat (daal and rice). Those words were like music to my ears. Now the next couple of hours were spent in Parvati's living room eating and continuing the conversation.

To be honest I was actually waiting for Shweta to leave but she was like a well-set Cheteshwar Pujara on a flat Indian pitch. Booked in for bed and breakfast. Impossible to get out. But I wasn't going to give up without trying. I asked to use the bathroom and stayed inside ten minutes longer than I needed to, hoping Shweta would leave. If she hadn't that was my que to take their leave. She hadn't. And it was time to say goodbye. Funnily enough Shweta also left at the same time as me. As if she was also waiting for me to leave.

To go home, I had to walk the same way those four boys had misbehaved with us and there was a chance I could bump into them on my way. That should have been the first and only thing on my mind. However, that thought didn't even cross my mind. I was giddy with happiness and almost floated my way home.

The next day me and Parvati texted each other on and off throughout the day. Then she called me around 5 pm while walking back home from the office and that phone call went on till 11 pm! I know!! It did cut off a couple of times like phone calls do after a certain while automatically, but one of us immediately called back and continued the conversation.

Next day at 5 p.m. I went to her office, which was also in the CBD, bang between both of our places. We met and, as we both were hungry, we went to a place called Hobson Indian Takeaway, my go-to place for home comforts. We packed up our parathas and went to her place. We also got an extra one for her flatmate Sakshi who was also from India.

When Sakshi came home, Parvati introduced us and said to Sakshi while pointing a finger at my face, "See it's there right? Do you see it too?"

Sakshi nodded in affirmation and both started laughing.

I was taken aback to say the least and asked Parvati what were they talking about.

"Your face," said Parvati, "it lights up naturally. It has a certain glow. I haven't seen it in anyone else's face apart from my own."

As any fully functioning adult who doesn't know how to react to compliments, I offered the classic awkward smile. Can never go wrong with the classics.

For the next few days, it became our routine. Every morning, I would walk her to her office, and we'd get coffee from the coffee shop opposite. One long black and one cappuccino with three and a half sugars. Then around 5pm I'd be back at the same coffee shop waiting for her. Then we'd grab a bite to eat and just walk around the Auckland CBD till we found a nice spot to sit. She absolutely hated PDA so obviously I would hold hands while walking and just give her a peck on her head or side-hug her every chance I got.

The main purpose of my stay in NZ at that time was a book I was writing. It was called *20 Women 20 Lives* and was set to be published on Women's Day 2020. Mike's publishing house Lasavia Publishing were going to publish that, and I was in fact staying with Mike and his lovely wife Leila at their beautiful Waiheke Island house at the time and only used to come to Auckland when I had cricket games to umpire. Yes, I was living the dream.

March 2020

Things back home, however, were not going as well. Mum had a health scare. Now my mom and I have an understanding. She would tell me whatever the situation was back home because not knowing what's going on at home can be the more stressful part. My elder brother, on the other hand, would always wait for the situation to get better before informing me.

So, when I got to know through a friend that Mum had to undergo an angiography, I wasn't worried because she had an angiography, I was worried because Mum hadn't told me, and we used to speak almost every day. I asked Mum about it on the phone, and she told me that she was admitted to the hospital and got the procedure done but there was nothing to worry about.

Still, I couldn't shake the feeling that something was not right and I needed to go back home. The feeling was too overwhelming. I couldn't ignore it. I spoke with Mike, and he said I should take the next flight home. Apart from the obvious family reasons, Mike and I had already discussed getting the book printed from India. And it will be a lot easier to get it done with me being there.

Lasavia usually got their books printed from Melbourne as it was cheaper than getting it done in NZ. To reduce the costs even more I had floated the idea when we started working on the book that we could print the copies from India as it will save us even more money. Mike was on board right away.

The only problem was Parvati. She had no idea about this as it all happened in the space of a day while she was at work. In the morning, we were speaking about which movies we are going to watch over the weekend and in the evening, I told her about me flying back to India. She first thought it was a joke. Then when she realised it wasn't, she felt betrayed. She thought this was in my plans all along, and I deliberately didn't inform her.

It was February 2020, and I was back in India. Mum was okay. No scares, phew! So, the plan for next few weeks was getting as many quotations about printing the book as I could before finalising the best option in consultation with Mike, while simultaneously looking for venues where we could hold the publishing event. As eight of the women in the book were from India, it made sense to publish the book there with their family and friends invited.

However, you know what they say, *you can plan as much as you want but it's only going to take one guy in China trying a different cuisine for it all to come crashing down.* Covid-19 hit. The world pressed a giant pause button. The book was indefinitely delayed. NZ PM Jacinda Ardern closed the borders. I couldn't do the one thing I came to India for, nor could I go back to New Zealand.

I had kept most of my stuff in New Zealand at Mike's Waiheke house. As it was just going to be a short visit to India for a couple of months at maximum, I just travelled with the small airbag that I carried with me from Waiheke to Auckland every time I stayed in

Auckland for a week or so to umpire some games. So I was in India, my stuff was on Waiheke Island and the girl who I had just fallen for was in Auckland, and so mad at me that she got a haircut. Apparently, it's what girls do.

Anyways, as a wise man said, "life makes sense backwards, but it must be lived forwards." And boy was I about to find it out.

One evening during the peak of Covid's first wave, I was in the upstairs bathroom when my brother came running up and knocked hard on the door, shouting "*Ajoba* (grandpa) has collapsed, come down right now!"

The scene downstairs was scary. Grandpa lay on the sofa, his hands and feet completely straight, his body stiff. My sister-in-law was rubbing his feet in a state of panic. My grandmother was trying to open his mouth as his teeth (artificial) had bitten on his tongue and kind of locked his jaw in such a way as he wasn't able to breathe. We were unable to open his mouth. My mother was on the phone to both her brothers crying and telling them to come to Aurangabad as soon as possible as the worst might have happened. My brother called for an ambulance.

I joined my grandmother in trying to open Grandpa's mouth. We succeeded. As soon as the mouth was open he let out a huge sigh. He was breathing. My brother and I decided to not wait for the ambulance, he brought the car around, and I do not know where I got the strength from, but I carried my grandfather from the living room couch to the car on the road. He usually weighs around 55-60 Kg, but he felt a lot more that night considering how stiff the body was.

We were on our way, with me and grandpa in the backseat. I could see only the right thumb and forefinger moving. The rest of his body seemed to be paralysed. So, I thought it could be a paralysis attack on the left side of the body. As soon as we reached the hospital, I asked the doctor at the emergency and casualty ward to put a catheter on grandpa as he had a history of being unable to pass urine and had undergone prostate surgery in the past. Looking at his stomach, which was swollen more than usual, we figured that could be the case again.

The doctor said nothing and went back to his cabin while the nurses settled grandpa on one of the beds. My brother got a call from the ambulance driver saying he has reached our place. My brother informed him we were already at the hospital! Grandpa was still the same, only his right thumb and forefinger could move. The rest of the body was still and stiff. From the doctor's office a nurse came and told us that the doctor has said we'd first have to do a Covid test before we can do anything else.

I didn't say anything to the nurse. Instead I barged into the doctor's office. "There's urine stuck in his bladder; you're going to put a catheter on him right now! Any tests you have to do you can do them later," I said.

I don't know whether it was the sternness in my voice or the fact that I was red with rage that made the doctor change his mind, but he came out with me and immediately instructed the nurses to bring a catheter.

The urine started passing as soon as the catheter was connected. And as the catheter filled up more and more with urine, the stiffness in my grandfather's body started going away. He moved both his feet and hands. And by the time the catheter was half full he opened his eyes.

A few minutes later the doctor spoke with us, and I apologised to him for my rude behaviour. A Few hours after that we were on our way home with grandpa and his catheter bag, which the doctor had asked us to keep for a week.

Soon Grandpa was back home, resting on his favourite spot on the sofa. Yes, my grandfather has a favourite spot on the sofa just like Sheldon Cooper. It is the corner spot on the far right of the sofa, not too dissimilar to his political stance. That spot is perfectly positioned in front of the TV while also giving him a view of the stairs going up to the bedroom, and a partial view of the kitchen to keep an eye for milk boiling over.

I watched him. His head resting on the sofa cushions, eyes closed. His *japmala* (loop of beads used for chanting) lay in his right hand, the only movement was his right thumb and forefinger moving the beads of the *japmala* as he chanted mantras in his mind.

We had just recovered from what happened to grandpa when my

uncle tested positive for covid. He was the eldest brother of my dad and they lived just two kilometres away. It goes without saying, they were very close. His whole family tested positive. Including his wife, son, daughter-in-law, and grandson.

We lost him just a few days later. Multiple organ failure, they said. His son was in the same hospital, undergoing treatment while his oxygen levels dropped to dangerous levels when Uncle died. We could not tell him that his father was no more because the doctors feared it might have an adverse impact on his health. He was discharged from hospital fifteen days later. Only then could we tell him what happened. He was devastated.

While recounting his hospital stay, he said the physical toll Covid took on his body was immense yet still bearable, but what he found incredibly hard to bear was the psychological toll of the decreasing number of patients in his Covid ward. They were not being shifted to the general ward, they were being shifted to the mortuary.

Three days later my own mother tested positive. When I took her to see the doctor, the doctor after doing the assessment asked her to wait outside while he spoke with me.

"Her blood pressure has shot up. I have given her the medication but considering her age I suggest you admit her in the Covid ward."

There was no way I was going to admit her to the Covid ward. I did not want her to go through the turmoil my cousin went through. Knowing my mother, I knew the best way for her to make a quick recovery was being at home being cared for by her family.

I informed the doctor of our decision.

He was hesitant. "It's your decision at the end of the day but bring her here immediately if her oxygen levels drop."

I did not tell Mum what the doctor had advised, nor did I tell my brother. My maternal uncle took both the grandparents to his place, we quarantined Mum in the upstairs ensuite bedroom, and decided that I'd be the only one caring for her to limit the spread.

We took every precaution, keeping her spirits high and in two weeks her tests came back negative. She made a full recovery. In fact, she gained a few kilos of weight as she had never rested for this long ever! Only after she had made a full recovery, did I tell the family what the doctor had suggested on the first day.

"Thank God," Mum said. "You didn't admit me to the hospital.

Over the next few months around twenty of my family members tested positive, including my brother and sister-in-law. Their symptoms were not as severe as Mum, and both made a full recovery quarantining at home. That's not to say it wasn't stressful.

The situation was same for every single one of my friends. No family was spared. And I'm not talking about just positive cases. I'm talking about deaths. Almost everyone I knew lost a loved one due to Covid. It was horrific. I dreaded texts from family and friends during Covid waves as they came bearing bad news. Someone is positive. Someone needs medication. Someone is on ventilator. Someone is no more.

I dreaded opening WhatsApp every morning. My social media timeline that used to be filled with requests was now full of people asking, pleading, begging, crying for their loved ones to be saved. At one point during the second wave, it felt as though there were no hospital beds for the living, and there was no space to bury the dead. People were saying cemeteries had run out of space in some places. While in others there was a 24-hour wait to cremate the dead. Multiple newspaper pages were filled with obituaries. Pictures of dead bodies floating on the Ganges River and hundreds more buried along the banks went viral. I even saw a video of a dog eating one of the dead bodies. Such was the pandemic that there was no respite even for the dead.

Scrolling social media was not for the faint-hearted during pandemic. Some of the hospitals had given up. Many hospitals which ran out of oxygen put out notices that if you wanted admission you had to arrange your own oxygen cylinder.

There are countless children who lost both parents. One sixteen-year-old boy from Bangalore lost both this parents and his only uncle in the space of two weeks. "I'm just 16, I don't know anything, what should I do" he posted. His post went viral on Reddit. It just completely broke me. Losing a loved one hurts but losing a loved one due to lack of resources knowing that had you been in a different city, a different hospital, they'd be alive... now that is trauma for a lifetime.

I have two friends that I blindly trust with my life. One is the first ever friend I made on my first day in school. His name is Rohit, now Major Rohit of the Indian Army, and just writing this swells my chest with pride. The second one I made a bit later when I was 10 and we'd just moved houses. Nilesh lived in the same housing society as us.

Rohit is the kind of person who I can rely on for telling me the truth. He'll never sugarcoat anything or tell me what I want to hear. He'll give me his honest opinion. He was the only person I called when I was in two minds if I should come to India or stay back in NZ. If I'm drowning, Rohit will first be the first one to jump in and pull me out of the water and then he'll also give me a proper slap for why I went in the water when I don't know how to swim, before proceeding to go save Nilesh. Because if I'm doing any stupid shit, there's no chance I'm doing it alone, Nilesh will always be there. Not just in doing stupid things but in general, Nilesh will always be in my corner. No questions asked, no judgements passed, Nilesh will be on my side.

It is no wonder these two were the best 'hoomans,' apart from family of course, as far as my Labrador-retriever Snoopy was concerned. They were her favourite people. When Snoopy was just a few months old and had a bad case of gastro and wasn't eating anything, she had become so weak we could literally see her bones. I used to take her to the vet twice a day for saline. But there was no improvement. She used to just lie in the house and not even move. Then one day Rohit came home, and seeing him, Snoopy got up from her place and walked towards him, her little tail wagging slowly with the little energy she had. That was the turning point and her health gradually improved until she made a full recovery. My mother and my grandmother would never tire of recounting that incident.

The next time Snoopy got seriously unwell was in late 2020. 2020 was really doing everything in its power to earn the title of worst year known to mankind. We went to the doctors, did a few tests, and it turned out snoopy had cancer. We had to get her operated on, get the cancer removed from her liver, and hope that it eased her pain and bought us a few more weeks with her. There was also a possibility of her not surviving the operation. Before they took her to the OT, I asked Nilesh who was with me at the hospital to take a picture of me and Snoopy. I knew that could be the last photo I had with her.

But she pulled through. The operation went well and Snoopy woke up. Although the operation had taken a lot out of her and she was no way out of danger yet, we were happy that we got to take her home. Snoopy had a very religious upbringing thanks to both of my grandparents. They were at home most of time and so was Snoopy and that ended up creating habits and rituals that became part of the daily life for the three of them.

Every morning my grandmother, for example, would be the first to wake up, take a bath and then go out in the front yard to pray and water the sacred Tulsi plant. Although little Snoopy would run around in excitement and bother Grandma a bit, the older Snoopy would just walk down the front steps and sit near the Tulsi plant as Grandma prayed.

Every evening my grandfather had a habit of walking in the front yard reciting the Changdev Pasashti. According to the internet, the Changdev Pasashti is a sixty-five-verse philosophical letter written by Saint Dyaneshwar to Yogi Changdev in 1291 CE. Containing the distilled version of the Upnishads (central religious texts of Hinduism), it is regarded by some as one of the finest primers on self-realization.

Every evening Snoopy would lie in the living room just chilling at the foot of the couch without a care in the world, but as soon as my grandfather got up to go outside, she would be out of the house before he had walked to the door. When she was little, she would take a ball in her mouth and go near Grandpa who would be walking back and forth reciting the Changdev Pasashti. Sometimes Grandpa would kick the ball away and she would fetch it. She would then settle down, sitting near the Tulsi plant and staying there however long it took for him to finish reciting the Changdev Pasashti.

So a normal day for Snoopy started with Vishnusahastranaam (thousand names of Lord Vishnu), recited by Grandma and ended with listening to the Changdev Pasashti recited by Grandpa. All while she sat near the sacred Tulsi plant.

Snoopy was home from hospital but there were no signs of improvement in her condition. She wouldn't drink water and eating was out of the equation. One positive though was that she was no longer growling in pain. She just lay there in her favourite spot in the living room. My brother and I took turns to sit with her through the night.

The next day was the same. She didn't eat anything, barely drank, and didn't move from her spot at all. In the evening, she started growling. We thought she must be hungry so I took some of her food in my hand and kept my hand near her mouth. She moved her mouth away. Again, I moved my hand closer to her mouth. She took a bite; it was the most reluctant bite I had ever seen. It was clear she didn't want to eat. The growling continued. I thought maybe she wanted to go outside, but as she had no energy, I carried her out to the front yard. I didn't get a good feeling about this.

I went inside and asked my brother to bring everyone to the front yard to pet Snoopy, to just sit with her. I called Nilesh and asked him to come home. By the time we got back out Snoopy had miraculously changed position. She was lying near the Tulsi plant. She could barely move. From where she drew the strength I don't know.

We all sat around her. My brother took her head in his lap. My baby niece came and patted her. So did Grandpa, Grandma, Mum, Sister-in-law, and Nilesh. Her breathing was getting slower and slower. In a few minutes it stopped. She was gone. My grandmother noticed how Snoopy was lying. Her head was to the north and her tail to the South. North-South is the position a body is kept in Hindu households after a person passes away. My family was heartbroken. So was Nilesh. Not a dry eye, except my own.

I didn't cry. We had to figure out what to do, where to bury her. I called up her doctor to inform she was no more and asked if he knew where we could bury her. He gave me contact details of a farm owner outside of the city and said we could bury her on his farm tomorrow. But somehow it didn't feel right to me. I trust my intuition a lot, even more than my intellect. If something seems like the logical thing to do but somehow it doesn't feel right, I won't do it.

I took Nilesh with me, and we went for a ride on my bike. I thought if I could get away from the grief, I would be able to think clearly. It was a cold winter night, and the roads were quiet. Neither of us had any place in mind that we could go. So, we just rode, turning whenever I felt like it, or going straight if I didn't feel like turning. A few minutes later we spotted a crematory. It was the same crematory at which my father had been cremated about 16 years back. I stopped the bike and turned to Nilesh.

"Should we ask here if they would bury Snoopy?"

"Unlikely they'll say yes. And high chance of them being offended too."

"Only one way to find out," I said and went ahead opening the cold metal gate of the crematory.

It was dead quiet inside. *Everyone must be asleep*, I thought. But then the dogs barked and woke the living up. A man came to meet us. His family managed the crematory and lived inside it.

I often wondered about the people managing these crematories, about the children growing up with death every day, listening to wails and cries of children who have lost parents and even worse parents who have lost children, knowing that their livelihood depends on someone's death. How can their hearts not become numb? Do they become as cold as the crematory's metal gate and even if you managed to break inside, there's no life left.

The man, Gajanan, greeted us and asked why we were there. I told him we had just lost our dog who was no less than a family member and that we would be indebted to him if he would let us bury her here in the same place I saw my father for the last time, a place I'd often driven by and remembered him, and now Snoopy too if he'd let us.

He agreed. He was a dog person as well, and they'd buried their dogs in their field just adjacent to the crematory. And asked us to come 5 a.m. the next morning saying that they would help us bury Snoopy. We thanked him quite a few times, took his phone number and came home.

Nilesh stayed with us, as my brother, Nilesh, and I just sat in the living room with the door open throughout the night and reminisced about Snoopy. Nilesh used to be shit scared of dogs, even puppies before Snoopy brought him on to the right side. Now he has a golden retriever of his own.

My grandmother stitched a garland for snoopy in the early hours of the morning and gave a few Tulsi leaves which she asked if we could place on Snoopy's head after we lowered her down. Then the three of us took Snoopy for her final drive.

Gajanan and his brothers had already dug up the grave, and had also arranged for some flowers. After Snoopy was lowered into the grave we all folded our hands and bowed down to her, including Gajanan and his brothers who threw flowers on Snoopy and then folded their hands. While we were leaving, Gajanan told us we can come back in a few days and plant a tree on that spot in her memory. It turned out the coldness at the crematory was just restricted to the metal gate. Inside, was filled with life and warmth.

How I Became the Secret King of Cricket Twitter

I have a very love-hate relationship with England. I will be forever grateful that people of a country, which gets five days of sunshine a year, managed to invent an outdoor sport that lasts five days, and which I love more than anything else. However, my blood absolutely boils when I think about how my people were introduced to the game – via the British Raj. The colonisation that lasted 200 years and took everything from my country. The psychological impact is still there to see.

> Until Rushdie and his followers arrived on the scene and made the intellectual ferment of modern India more visible to the outsider, India remained, in the dominant

grids of Western perceptions, a place of 'heat and dust' where the Europeans had once founded a resplendent raj. To 'heat and dust' was often added another familiar list: of crowds, dirt and diseases.

I was just a month old when these words were published in the *Economic and Political Weekly*, the writer – Dipesh Chakrabarty.

I love the English language but hate how my country is depicted in it in the Western media. India suffers from massive colonial hangover. And it's there to see in every walk of life. I'll talk about cricket as I have experienced the colonial hangover in cricket first hand. In fact, I was a prime example of colonial hangover in cricket myself thanks to the media, which shaped my thoughts.

I believed wins in India did not matter. I rated overseas wins more, especially those achieved in SENA countries. SENA is an acronym the Indian cricket community uses for matches played in and against South Africa, England, New Zealand, and Australia. There's a bigger respect your team and the players earn in the cricket world if they perform there.

On the flip side, they are not considered to be great players if they have an average record in England. Virat Kohli is a great example. He had a horrible tour of England in 2014, and had he not scored in England on his next tour in 2018 there would always have been a question mark over his greatness because he failed to score in one particular country.

Such a question mark is never put in front of England or Australian players. Take the example of Ricky Ponting who Virat Kohli is often compared to due to his similar aggressive batting style and combative captaincy style. Ponting is considered an all-time great. One could also make a case of him being arguably the greatest batter to play the sport. No one would raise an eyebrow. Now this despite Ponting averaging just 26 in India in Test cricket, almost half of his career average of 51.85 and having scored just one hundred in 14 attempts in India. No one mentions his record in India.

The same applies to great England players with a poor record on the subcontinent, which is never mentioned in the English media.

One thing about English cricket, no matter how strong their cricket has been at a particular point, their media has been stronger. They set the narratives, and the rest of the cricket world follows.

Indian media is no exception. They'll ask any Tom, Dick or Harry who has played for England a few times, about their views on Virat Kohli's technique and their opinion will make headlines all over the country. Brad Hogg who was a former Australian spin bowler would tweet something about Rohit Sharma's batting and a snap of that tweet will be in the newspapers in India the next day.

You'll never see any English or Australian journalist or media channel ask Sunil Gavaskar, one of the all-time great opening batsmen, his opinion on the failings of Aussie or English openers. Even if Mr. Gavaskar were to give his opinion on an Indian news channel, that comment would never make the newspapers back in England and Australia.

My ancestors' fight was against the Englishman's sword. My fight was against his word. I did not care if we managed to change their opinions about my country. All I wanted to do was to change the opinions of my people about our own country. To have some pride. They should take pride in the performance of Team India at home too, and not just in SENA countries. England and Australia never demean their team wins at home. And Test cricket in India is no less important than that in England or Australia.

It's not that difficult to understand England's struggle in accepting the current world order in cricket. Because the game that began as an idyllic pastime for the elites in imperial England is now a commercial sport for the masses dominated by one of its former colonies – India. India's domestic T20 competition, the Indian Premier League is the biggest league in cricket and one of the biggest in world sport.

Before the IPL came about, every amateur/professional cricketer in the world used to dream about going to England to ply their trade in county cricket in April-May. However, things have changed. Now every professional and semi-professional cricketer in the world dreams about going to India to play in the IPL in April-May.

Kevin Pietersen was one of the first English cricketers to participate in the IPL. And he faced a lot of criticism at the time in the British press for it. When he was first bought in the IPL for a whopping 1.55 million dollars by the Royal Challengers Bangalore in 2009, *The Times* published an article with the headline – 'Kevin Pietersen: Dumbslog Millionaire'.

When India defeated England in a Test at Ahmedabad in February 2021 that finished inside two days with spinners taking the bulk of the wickets, Indian cricketer R Ashwin was involved in a heated exchange with an English journalist who asked Ashwin whether he thought the pitch was a good cricket surface.

> What makes a good surface? Who defines this? Seam on the first day and then bat well and then spin on the last two days? Come on! Who makes all these rules? We need to get over it and not talk about whatever picture you want to paint.
>
> If you are asking if it is a good Test surface, I don't see any of the players coming from England having an issue with the surface. They want to improve; they look like they want to have a contest. Is it the (past) players and the people who are reporting back that want their players to not compete and complain about the pitches? Because we have never done that on any of the tours.

What Ashwin was not so subtly saying was that pitches that behave differently than the traditional English pitches are good cricket pitches as well.

More than a year later when 17 wickets fell on day one of the England v New Zealand Test at Lord's, former Indian cricketer Wasim Jaffer posted this tweet:

> When 17 wkts fall in a day at Lord's, talk is about skills of the bowlers.
> When 17 wkts fall in a day at Ahmedabad, talk is about conditions.

Wasim's tweet and the interaction between R Ashwin and an English journalist are great examples of what, historian and post-colonial scholar, Dipesh Chakrabarty calls, 'returning the gaze,' i.e. returning the gaze of western science by making the colonizer a subject of inquiry from the colonized.

It's now time to let you guys in on a little secret. You know the tweet mentioned above posted by Indian cricketer Wasim Jaffer? It was posted by Mr. Jaffer, but it was a brainchild of yours truly. I had been managing Mr. Jaffer's social media.

I met Mr. Jaffer in August 2019 in Mumbai for the first time, after sliding into his DMs on Twitter saying I have some ideas about his social media and that if he was interested, I'd love to meet and discuss. To my own surprise, he agreed. I had zero experience of running celebrity social media accounts, but what I lacked in experience I made up for in passion, and I'm forever grateful to Mr. Jaffer for seeing it.

It didn't take long for me to convince him. He had already seen the double standards Indian cricketers were subjected to by the English media. Heck, he had even been on the receiving end of it. I told him about the fan aspect as well. How plenty of English ex cricketers and journalists have built a following on Twitter just by giving sarcastic replies to poor Indian fans who end up taking their words literally and then get made fun of for their poor English.

It's not the fans' fault. English is probably their third language. And English is not a measure of intelligence anyway, and they shouldn't feel bad about it at all, let alone made to feel inferior by a former England cricketer with a million followers who can only speak one language. I can bet you that cricket fan with poor English is more updated about the current game than any ex-cricketer who has become a pundit based simply on reputation.

I managed to convince Mr. Jaffer that Indian cricket needed a leader on Twitter that would stand up for Indian cricket and the fans as well. That would give back to the English ex-players and media in their own words as our battle was against the Englishmen's words. And I told him if we were to do that, Indian cricket Twitter will rally behind us, and we'll be the best account on cricket Twitter. He laughed at the last part, but he was on board.

Take a look at this tweet from former Australian cricketer Brad Hogg before the first Test between India and Australia. Hogg wasn't a top order batter. He was a spinner who batted at number nine. But here he is giving *gyaan* (Hindi for Knowledge) to the Indian top order on how to play.

Brad Hogg ✓
@Brad_Hogg

Indian top order need to know where their off stump is, learn to leave the ball off a good length, and not chase the ball moving away outside off stump.
#HoggysTips #AUSAvIND

7:06 PM · 12 Dec 20

36 Reposts **49** Quotes **2,367** Likes

Fair enough. He is entitled to his opinions and to post it on social media. But so are we.

Wasim Jaffer ✓
@WasimJaffer14

Australia need to know who their top order is 😏 #AusvInd

Brad Hogg ✓ @Brad_Hogg · 12 Dec 20
Indian top order need to know where their off stump is, learn to leave the ball off a good length, and not chase the ball moving away outside off stump.
#HoggysTips #AUSAvIND

7:41 PM · 12 Dec 20

887 Reposts **253** Quotes **13.8K** Likes

Unlike Brad Hogg, Wasim Jaffer was a top order bat. This tweet went viral as Australia actually didn't know who was going to open the innings for them in the first Test due to one of their regular openers being injured and the other being out of form.

When it comes to belittling India's wins at home and unfairly criticising what are standard Indian cricket pitches, Aussie media is sometimes as bad as the English one, especially when their team is losing. And we had to call it out.

Wasim Jaffer ✔
@WasimJaffer14

😉 pc: @MarsCuriosity #INDvAUS #BGT2023

1:30 AM · 09 Feb 23 · **1.4M** Views

2,646 Reposts   **103** Quotes   **45.8K** Likes

Wasim Jaffer ✓
@WasimJaffer14

Pretty sure India didn't prepare wickets in Australia in 2020-21 and 2018-19, Mr. Healy :) #INDvAUS #BorderGavaskarTrophy

 **Mufaddal Vohra** ✓ @mufad... · 04 Feb 23

Ian Healy said, "if India produces fair wickets, Australia will win BGT. If it's rank turners, India will win".

3:52 AM · 05 Feb 23 · **697K** Views

872 Reposts **28** Quotes **13.1K** Likes

Wasim Jaffer ✓
@WasimJaffer14

Simon, reason why Ahmedabad pitch only favoured one team is cos England picked 4 pacers on a turning pitch 😅

> 🐦 **simon hughes** ✓ @theanaly... · 19 Dec 22
>
> To all @BCCI cricket fans - yes the Gabba pitch was an unfair contest between bat and ball - look at the dints in the surface created by it being too green and damp at the start - but it DIDN'T especially favour one side. #A...

Post your reply

The below interaction with former England captain Michael Vaughan remains one of my favourites. It happened after England had beaten India in the T20 World Cup semifinal in 2022.

Michael Vaughan ✔
@MichaelVaughan

So @WasimJaffer14 .. Your forfeit .. You must film yourself singing 'Jos Buttler's Barmy army' and post on here please .. Unlucky .. it was a close game 😛😛😛 #ICCWorldCup2022

11:58 PM · 10 Nov 22

618 Reposts **37** Quotes **12.1K** Likes

Wasim Jaffer ✔
@WasimJaffer14

I see you're having a ball on here 😄 And fair enough too, England were superb 👏 But I'm not following you.. I don't recall agreeing to film anything.. and please help me here, I know Jos Buttler, but what's a Barmy army? #INDvENG #T20WorldCup

> 🖼 Michael Vaughan ✔ @Mich... · 10 Nov 22
> So @WasimJaffer14 .. Your forfeit .. You must film yourself singing 'Jos Buttler's Barmy army' and post on here please .. Unlucky .. it was a close game 😛😛😛 #ICCWorldCup2022

5:26 AM · 11 Nov 22

285 Reposts **4** Quotes **7,442** Likes

Michael took the "I'm not following you" part literally. And posted a screenshot that showed Wasim Jaffer follows him on Twitter. And then we ended up teaching the Englishman some English.

Wasim Jaffer ✔
@WasimJaffer14

I don't follow   🐦 f

It means i dont understand.

when youre "following" someone during a conversation it means you understand what they are saying or where theyre going with a story. when you dont follow it means youre lost- what they are saying doesnt make sense to you.

Michael Vaughan ✔ @Mich... · 11 Nov 22

Post your reply   📷

England remained our favourite team/country to make fun of because they know how to take a joke, and in fact no one makes fun of England as much as English people themselves. So, there was no risk of our tweet being taken out of context. And we used that advantage to full effect. Just before the T20 WC in 2022 there was brief period when England were without a Prime Minister. Liz Truss had just resigned, and Rishi Sunak was yet to be named her successor. And comedy, like batting, is all about timing.

Wasim Jaffer ✓
@WasimJaffer14

Was doing a SWOT analysis for T20 WC participating teams and realised:

India don't have a 150K+ bowler.
Pak don't have a seasoned finisher.
NZ don't have a great record in Aus.
SL don't have an experienced squad.
England don't have a Prime Minister.
#T20worldcup22 #LizTruss

3:17 AM · 21 Oct 22

2,119 Reposts   **166** Quotes   **38.5K** Likes

When India obliterated South Africa in a game coincidently played on the birth anniversary of the great Mahatma Gandhi, we posted the following tweet. Now for those who are still unaware about Mahatma Gandhi, and his connection to South Africa, in short if you're American, Gandhi led the non-violence movement against the British rule in India and had spent 21 years in South Africa where he developed his political views, ethics, and politics.

Wasim Jaffer ✓
@WasimJaffer14

Violence?
On Gandhi Jayanti?
Against South Africa?! #INDvSA

3:57 AM · 03 Oct 22

2,579 Reposts   **179** Quotes   **42.6K** Likes

Schooling the Western media about how to report on India cricket remained the meat and potatoes of our Twitter account.

Wasim Jaffer ✓
@WasimJaffer14

Captain Courageous: World applauds as Virat Kohli's team brings dead game to life and scripts historic win.
Here fixed it for you @FoxCricket.
#ENGvIND

🏏 **Fox Cricket** @FoxCricket · 07 Sep 21

'Classless': World divided as Virat Kohli trolls Barmy Army after embarrassing England

👉 bit.ly/3kXFyPL

6:46 PM · 07 Sep 21

Wasim Jaffer ✓
@WasimJaffer14

Fixed it for you @TelegraphSport
#AUSvsIND #Rahane

6:11 AM · 28 Dec 20

3,569 Reposts **216** Quotes **43.1K** Likes

Although calling out the English double standards and standing up for India was the heart of our social media strategy, it wasn't all we did. We started using memes to react to cricket matches and it became an instant hit. It was early 2020 and memes had already become the language of the common man, but it wasn't common to see Indian cricketers post memes on social media.

Our memes were so loved that people started calling Wasim Jaffer a meme lord. Even *Wisden* couldn't help but take notice. They did a whole piece titled – 'Wait when did Wasim Jaffer get so good at Twitter?' That piece was a collection of our memes and it ended with this line, "And so, we've the biggest find, by far, of IPL 2020 – Wasim

Jaffer, the meme lord".

Then we took it up a notch. Before an important game, I'd ask Mr. Jaffer what changes he'd like to see in the team and then proceed to post a coded tweet tagging the Indian captain on match day, asking fans to decode it in the comments.

For example, the tweet below, asking Indian captain Ajinkya Rahane to pick Gill and Rahul (first letter of every word) for the next test after India faced an embarrassing defeat in the first Test in which they were bowled out for 36 runs – their lowest ever total.

Wasim Jaffer ✔
@WasimJaffer14

Dear @ajinkyarahane88, here's a (hidden) message for you. Good luck for Boxing Day!

People
In
Cricket
Know
Grief
In
Life
Lingers
Aplenty
Never
Dabble
Rise
And
Handcraft
Unique
Legacy

PS: you guys are open to have a go and decode the msg too 😉
#INDvsAUS #AUSvIND

Post your reply   📷

And then there was this one suggesting the batting order India should play.

As you can see Twitter user Yo Yo Funny Singh accurately decoded the message. KL Rahul unfortunately got injured but Shubman Gill was picked and ended up playing a defining role as India made a stunning come back to win the series.

Wasim Jaffer had 1800 Twitter followers when we started working together. Now he has 1.3 million Twitter followers, 320,000 Instagram followers, and over 20,000 subscribers on YouTube. We never spent a single penny on promoting any of those accounts. It was just me and him working together to create content that would resonate with the fans.

During peak covid we used our Twitter to amplify help requests. We received hundreds of help requests daily and it was my job to verify them, and to repost them on our page with local authorities tagged to ensure quick action.

Our tweets had a massive psychological impact. Indian fans started calling out UK and Aussie media for their double standards. Foreign cricketers who used to make fun of broken English of Indian cricket fans by giving sarcastic replies stopped doing it altogether.

Michael Vaughan, the chief troller of Indian cricket came so far along that he's now a chief supporter, defending Indian cricketers on social media against their arch-rivals Pakistan. Although if it wasn't for Michael's ancestors there would be no Pakistan.

Michael Vaughan ✔
@MichaelVaughan

Come on @MHafeez22 !!! India have hammered 8 teams playing great cricket .. @imVkohli now has 49 tons and his last was an anchor role innings on a tricky pitch .. His team won by over 200 !!!! This is utter nonsense .. #CWC2023 #India #Pakistan

🎙 **Immy|| 🇮🇳** ✔ @TotallyImro45 · 06 Nov 23
Mohammad Hafeez. 'I saw sense of selfishness in Virat Kohli's batting and this happened for the third time in this World Cup. In the 49th over, he was looking to take a single to reach his own hundred and he di...

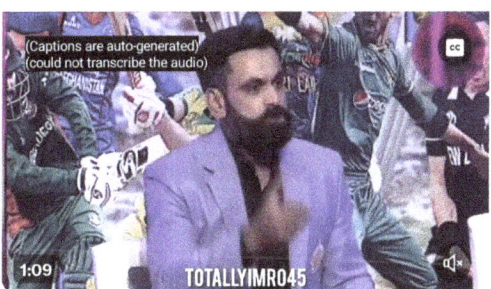

(Captions are auto-generated) (could not transcribe the audio)

cc

1:09   TOTALLYIMRO45

3:45 PM · 07 Nov 23 · **3.7M** Views

Full Circle

To those of you still patiently wondering what happened with Parvati, thank you for sticking around. This chapter is for you.

After I came back to India in early 2020 Parvati and I tried the long-distance thing for a few months, but it didn't work as there was too much happening in both of our lives and with Corona and border closure we didn't know if or when we'd see each other again. So, we decided to put a pin in it for the time being.

I did one important thing though. I called her mother and told her that me and Parvati might not be together, but when in the future she thinks about finding a good match for her daughter just think about me, and if possible, give me a call.

And... she did. A couple of years later when Parvati was in India the call flashed on my mobile. I knew what the call was about. I was ready. You know how they say *when you truly want something the whole universe conspires to bring that to you*. That's exactly how I felt at that time. The New Zealand border had also fully opened, and although my visa had expired, I received another work visa from Immigration New Zealand to make up for the work visa I had lost due to the border closure. I was going back to Aotearoa.

The first person I called after I got my visa was heartbroken with the news. He was Mr. Joshi of a reputed blood bank in my city. My blood group (O Negative) is rare so I try to donate as much as I can. One time after donating blood, I asked Mr. Joshi which patient was going to get my blood. He said it is for an eight-year-old girl called Anushka who suffers from thalassemia and requires a blood transfusion every month.

He then asked if I would I like to be her permanent donor, which would mean donating blood every three months at their blood bank and only for Anushka. I couldn't say no to that. And so I became one of Anushka's permanent donors. While filling out the form, the staff at the blood bank wrote my name as Virat, instead of Viraj. I didn't correct them. So, for the next three years Virat donated blood to Anushka every three months. That's why Mr Joshi was the first person I called as I knew he'd need time to find a replacement donor. It wouldn't be easy to find another Virat for Anushka.

The bottom line is I got my visa, and just like that we were married and back in New Zealand. We lived in the same apartment complex I had dropped her off at the first night we met. The money I was making at the time managing Mr. Jaffer's social media accounts was more than enough for me, as a single bachelor, to live a comfortable life in India. Unfortunately it wasn't enough for a married man in New Zealand. Thus, before we got married, I made a promise to Parvati's father that the first thing I'ld do when we got to New Zealand is get a stable 9-5.

I had never worked 9-5 in my life. All of my life so far was about doing what I loved, following my dreams and basically getting paid to watch cricket at home. It was pretty sweet. I woke up and chose to do whatever I wanted to do on that particular day. And trust me I knew how fortunate I was.

They say *lucky are those who get time to follow their intellectual curiosity and luckier are those who get paid to follow their intellectual curiosity*. But deep down wc all know that *luckiest are those who get an afternoon nap daily*. I was all of the three, all throughout my twenties, but it was time for a change and I was ready. I love a challenge of doing something new, something different.

My life had come such a full circle that at this point doing something different meant doing the normal 9-5. It took me a couple of months to find a job and couple of months is exactly how long I stayed in that job. Because, and to paraphrase Dwight Schrute, *I'm nothing if not a loyal employee*. I value loyalty the most. And if I found another organisation that valued loyalty more than the organisation I was with, I would be loyal to them.

So, I joined a new organisation as they valued my loyalty much more than my first company. At the time of writing, I still work there. It is a healthcare organisation. I look after the Hawkes Bay region. My job is basically to make sure that we provide enough support to ensure the palliative patients can spend their last few weeks, sometimes days, living at home with their family, rather than in a hospital or hospice. Yes, I'm doing God's work so maybe I'll go to Heaven. However, I'm a Hindu. It's not as simple as Heaven and Hell for us. We have a small thing called rebirths. So, I must factor in that as well. I hope I accrue enough good karma to at least be born as a white male in my next birth. It would be good to do life on easy mode for a change.

You know what's the next best thing to being a white male? Having a white passport. And by white passport I mean having a passport that could give you rights such as visa free travel to Europe or a working holiday visa. A working holiday visa is what us mere mortals, and by mere mortals I mean people who are always stopped at "random" security checks at airports, dream of. *The lucky bugger is going to have a white passport* was one of the first thoughts that came to my mind when we found out Parvati was pregnant. And what a day to find it out too - the 17th of July, my late dad's birthday.

So here I was doing a 9-5 that had nothing to do with cricket at all. I couldn't be further from cricket as New Zealand's time zone makes it incredibly hard for me to follow cricket. For the first time in my life I was missing cricket matches, and you know what? I didn't care. At all.

The satisfaction of being able to provide for my family was so huge that I didn't care what I did as long as the rent was paid, there was food in the fridge and laughter in the house. It is what makes the world go round. The innate desire of a man to provide for his family. For my dad the desire was so strong that he ended up doing in just 40 years of life what most people do in 60. And not just in terms of earning material wealth but also in terms of name and legacy. Just being Rajendra Deshpande's son opened many doors for me and my brother.

While my life was going on a steady upward curve, the NZ economy however, was going in a downward curve and entering a recession. People were getting laid off, even Parvati wasn't spared; she lost her job and was devastated. I told her not to worry about getting another job and just focus on her health and wellbeing during pregnancy and even afterwards for however long she needs. I'll take care of the financial side. With my job and social media side hustle, we were financially stable.

We decided it was good for her to spend a few months in India being looked after by her parents and also my family had organised a grand babyshower for her. I surprised her with a pair of diamond earrings as a gift and was virtually present during the entire ceremony on video call. She looked so happy and was glowing. I needed to see that happy celebration of a new life we were about to bring into the world because, just earlier that day, we were told in a meeting that my company was going to implement a restructure, after which there would be no Onboarding Team. And the tasks the Onboarding Team does were going to be divided to two different teams. I wouldn't have given a rat's ass about this if I hadn't been a part of the Onboarding Team.

This thing affected me on multiple levels. My visa was about to expire in three months and I was going to renew it with the help of my company. The two teams our Onboarding Team was going to be merged into were two different teams with different pays. There were six positions available in the team with higher pay (joining this would automatically extend my visa for a further three years and put me on a pathway to residency).

Whereas joining the other team with lesser pay would mean I would still have a job for the next three months till my visa expires but would then have to pack my bags and go back to India.

Every single one of my 30-memeber Onboarding Team was going to apply for the 6 positions available in the team two levels up from us. And those who don't get selected would be accommodated in the team a level down from us. At this time I had only been in the organisation for three months, I was among the newest members of the Onboarding Team and had to compete against my friends and colleagues who had been doing this job for many years.

All this was in my mind while I was on a video call virtually attending my wife's baby shower the same evening. Of course, I was not going to share with my pregnant wife the distressing news of my team being disbanded.

And also, this was nothing I couldn't handle by myself. I've been through this exact same thing before when I was stuck in India and lost entirety of my post study work visa due to Covid. I didn't sit and sulk. I took action and ended up creating a new income source from scratch by managing social media account of the former Indian cricketer. And it's still going strong.

I know I thrive in adversity. That's a family trait, one I'll tell you about soon. I thrive in adversity so much that I think I attract it. However there hasn't been a single adversity in my life after which I hadn't levelled up. Every time I felt like I was buried it turned out that I was in fact planted. And I take that 'when has it ever not worked out for me' attitude towards all aspects of my life. To understand where this attitude in me comes from I need to take you back in time.

Aai (Mum)

"Today in broad daylight a Brahmin (priest) will be murdered!"

"Today in broad daylight a Brahmin will be murdered!"

A mad man with blood thirst was walking around a remote village in Western India some 50 years ago, shouting this as he passed through the small, dusty lanes, making the whole village aware of his intentions.

There was no doubt who his target was, for there was only one Brahmin house in that small village. This was his way of warning the Brahmin man to either leave the village forever or be ready to leave the planet.

For if any of those outcomes happened, that mad man would have his hands on the huge piece of land that belonged to the Brahmin man's mother, a piece of land that the mad man and his five brothers were tasked to look after.

They had their eyes on the land all along and were just waiting for that old lady to pass away. Her husband had died when her sons were six, eight, and ten. She was an incredibly courageous woman. She had to be because she had the biggest piece of land in the village and she was the only house of her caste in that village. Houses were segregated as per castes at that time in India. In some places, it still happens.

She also had the biggest heart. Opened the coffers to the entire village during drought without a second thought. The entire village looked at her like a mother, except the family that was tasked to look after her land. They were after her land. Her oldest son was an engineer in a big city; the second one was a Cost and Works accountant and had secured a really good job in a big city. The third one was staying with her but he was handicapped. The mad-man didn't consider him a threat.

However, when the woman was getting old, her middle son decided to leave his high-paying job and take his newly married wife back with him to the village to look after his ageing mother and handicapped brother. He ensured the brother got a job in the local post office and was married to a wonderful girl who saw past his disability. And then he made it his life's mission to look after and preserve the land that's been in his family for generations.

That land had his family's name on it. He wouldn't let someone whose job was to just look after what belonged to his family take it as if it's theirs. Not on his watch.

That man was my grandfather (Mum's father). And he was sitting in his house that day with my grandmother as the mad man deliberately passed their house multiple times shouting, "Today in broad daylight a Brahmin will be murdered!"

A few hours later, that mad man banged on my grandfather's door. His voice had reached fever pitch now. The entire village had come outside, but no one dared to stop him. My grandfather got up from his chair, walked calmly towards the door, and opened the door.

The mad man was right in front of him. His eyes big and red with blood thirst, and he had a big koyta knife in his right hand, which is used to cut sugarcane.

My grandfather looked at that man and smiled. That's it. He looked in the eyes of death and smiled and held that gaze. After what seemed to be the longest two minutes, the mad man walked away.

I would often ask my grandfather about that incident and particularly that period in his life. How did he get through it? The answer he'd give wasn't as satisfactory for the teenage me growing up. He had a simple motto that he said got him through everything in life: Yeh bhi din jayenge (this too shall pass). For the teenage me, it couldn't get more cliché than that. I expected a heroic answer, but as I grew up, I realised clichés are clichés for a reason. Because they work.

My grandfather also had a secret weapon, my grandmother. The toughest and the softest woman I've known. And the children they raised ended up being a living proof of their values. My mother is the eldest child; she has two younger brothers.

When my dad passed away, the older of my mum's brothers met with an accident while he was with his family on the way to meet us. Both he and his wife were critically injured, and they were worried he wouldn't survive. Fortunately, both his kids were safe.

Now imagine this situation from the younger brother's point of view. Your elder sister has just lost her husband, and you're there to support her family, and then you hear the news that your elder brother's family were in a highway accident and he's fighting for his life.

Add to that, in a month's time, you have the most important exam of your life (He was a practicing lawyer studying to become a judge and had one final attempt left before his age would make him ineligible to sit for the exam).

My youngest mama (maternal uncle) would divide his days between a hospital in Mumbai (where the eldest mama and his wife were admitted after their accident) and our home in Aurangabad. He would study during the night in a bathroom as he didn't want to disturb anyone else. He passed the exam in his final attempt, and as I write this, he's been a respected judge in the Indian Judiciary for over two decades.

My eldest mama, who was battling for his life, made a full recovery. For the longest time, they were worried he might lose his vision; he still has some trouble when looking at things slightly above his peripheral vision from his right eye.

He couldn't work for a few years while he was recovering. He literally had to start from scratch. Imagine starting from scratch after you've done the hard yards and climbed the corporate ladder to the very top. Like landing on a snake in snakes and ladders that leaves you back at square one.

And then, through sheer willpower and hard work, climbing that ladder again so high that now your skills are in demand all over the world, and you pick and choose how long you want to work for and in which country, and just work from there for a couple of months and come back home.

I just need to look around my own house, and I see stories of people overcoming adversity. I don't even have to leave the house for that. My elder brother was just 15 when dad passed away. His first reaction upon learning that our dad was no more, mum would later tell me, was he was worried about me as he thought I was too young to face this.

He wasn't too old either; he was just 15, touching 16, but even on the darkest day of his life, my brother thought about my wellbeing first. And that sums him up for me. Always putting his family above his own self. He learned to drive our car in two days, yes, two days. So he could drive mum to work. I saw him become a man overnight. He ensured my childhood was extended for a few years, even though that meant sacrificing his teenage years.

My dad's side of the family came from nothing. Seven brothers and four sisters built their life from scratch, sticking together through thick and thin. Embodiment of that Kipling quote - "For the strength of the Pack is the Wolf, and the strength of the Wolf is the Pack".

My dad was the wolf of the family. The amount of grief my dad's family experienced after his passing can't be measured. I never even thought about it while growing up. I was so focused on my own loss that I didn't once think that yes, I have lost my dad but the people around me have also lost a close loved one who cared for them and protected them. My older aunts and uncles lost a younger brother they looked after like their own kid and the younger ones lost an older brother who looked after them like they were his own kids. My cousins lost their favourite uncle.

I wonder if they ever got to express their grief for internally they must have thought what's their grief compared to what my mother, my brother and I were going through. What I do know is we felt incredibly loved and protected from them. Well maybe that's how that grief was expressed, for what is grief but love preserving.

They taught me the meaning of family and of sticking together and looking after your loved ones. And how there's nothing more important. And now I was about to have a small family of my own. I wasn't going to let small things like recession and a work visa that was about to expire stop me from providing for my family. My grandfather saw death in the face and smiled. I'm the same flesh and blood. And now the blood of all my ancestors, through me, had a chance to fight for their newest member.

And the odds being against me had already made me the ideal candidate because no one wanted it more than me. Others were fighting to stay in the company whereas I came equipped with the unfair advantage of the unwavering determination of a soon to be father who was fighting to stay in the country his son was about to be born in. No one else had a chance.

On 28th February 2024 I got that promotion. Which also meant my visa which was going to expire on 8th April 2024 was now extended for three more years. My son was born on 8th March 2024. And this is the first time my family is finding out what I was actually going through during those couple of months (that is if they bother to read this far).

When my son was born I wished dad was here to experience this moment. To experience that his son is now a father himself. That his thoughts, his values, his persona, his humour, his kindness, his bravado, his big heartedness, his legacy, his name is going to be carried forward.

The book was going to end at the above paragraph. After writing it I glanced over at my phone. My wallpaper is my baby boy on my mother's lap looking up at her. It's my favourite photo of him. Then it hit me. My father had been with me, with us, all along. In the form of my mother. She had ensured our lives turned out to be exactly how they would have turned out had he been around.

Imagine your father right now. Now consciously imagine the safety net he provides just by being there. *It's okay Dad will take care of it*, is such a powerful thought. It's such a powerful thought that can give you so much confidence that you're ready to take on the world. And when a boy loses his father, the first thing he loses is that confidence.

My mother ensured both me and my brother never lost that confidence because she was there. She gave us the freedom to pursue our dreams. And she was always there to catch us if we fell. She was and is our safety net. If I asked her for 5,000 rupees, she would send 10,000. I mean, what's more father-like behaviour than that?

She did every single thing that a father is supposed to do while already being the best mother anyone could ask for. We were never told things along the line of *we would have done that thing if your father were alive*. It was never, "we would have gotten a dog if you father was here," but, "your father would have loved playing with Snoopy". It was never, "If your father was here, we would have sent you to New Zealand for study", but, "Your father would have booked his and my flight tickets and we would have surprised you at your graduation in New Zealand."

What it subconsciously did was we never missed Dad during a difficult phase but always remembered him when we were happy. Like I am at this very moment finishing this book. Because I know that as happy as I am, he is up there, happier for me.

www.ingramcontent.com/pod-product-compliance
Lightning Source LLC
Chambersburg PA
CBHW051317120626
46547CB00015B/2283